U.S. Department of Justice
Office of Justice Programs
810 Seventh Street N.W.
Washington, DC 20531

Alberto R. Gonzales
Attorney General

Regina B. Schofield
Assistant Attorney General

David W. Hagy
Deputy Assistant Attorney General, Office of
Justice Programs and Principal Deputy Director,
National Institute of Justice

This and other publications and products of the National Institute
of Justice can be found at:

National Institute of Justice
www.ojp.usdoj.gov/nij

Office of Justice Programs
Partnerships for Safer Communities
www.ojp.usdoj.gov

JAN. 07

Investigations Involving the Internet and
Computer Networks

NCJ 210798

 NIJ

David W. Hagy
Deputy Assistant Attorney General,
Office of Justice Programs and Principal Deputy Director,
National Institute of Justice

This document was prepared under Interagency Agreement #2003–IJ–R–029 between the National Institute of Justice and the National Institute of Standards and Technology, Office of Law Enforcement Standards.

The National Institute of Justice is a component of the Office of Justice Programs, which also includes the Bureau of Justice Assistance, the Bureau of Justice Statistics, the Office of Juvenile Justice and Delinquency Prevention, and the Office for Victims of Crime.

Photo Credits

Cover: Getty Images and Photodisc
Text: Photodisc, Getty Images, and Digital Stock

Foreword

As the use of the Internet and other computer networks has grown rapidly in recent years, so has the opportunity for electronic crime. Unlawful activity can be committed or facilitated online. Criminals can trade and share information, mask their identity, identify and gather information on victims, and communicate with co-conspirators. Web sites, electronic mail, chat rooms, and file sharing networks can all yield evidence in an investigation of computer-related crime.

This report was developed by the Technical Working Group for the Investigation of High Technology Crimes and is intended to be a resource for individuals responsible for investigations involving the Internet and other computer networks. It is one of a series of electronic crime investigation documents already published or in development by the National Institute of Justice (NIJ). The guides are developed by technical working groups that consist of practitioners and subject matter experts brought together by NIJ to help law enforcement agencies and prosecutors deal with the growing volume and complexity of electronic crime.

The series of guides will discuss the investigation process from the first responder, to the laboratory, to the courtroom. Specifically, the guides will address:

- Electronic crime scene investigation by first responders.

- Forensic examination of digital evidence.

- Internet and network investigations.

- Investigative uses of technology.

- Courtroom presentation of digital evidence.

- Development of a digital evidence forensic unit.

The recommendations presented in this guide are not mandates or policy directives and may not represent the only correct course of action. The guide is intended to be a resource for those who investigate crimes related to the Internet and other computer networks. It does not discuss all of the issues that may arise in these investigations and does not attempt to cover traditional investigative procedures.

NIJ extends its appreciation to the members of the Technical Working Group for the Investigation of High Technology Crimes for their involvement. We commend them for the long hours of work required to prepare this report and recognize that they did this while still performing their existing duties with their home offices or agencies. Their commitment of time and expertise was invaluable to the success of the project.

David W. Hagy
Deputy Assistant Attorney General,
Office of Justice Programs and
Principal Deputy Director,
National Institute of Justice

Technical Working Group for the Investigation of High Technology Crimes

Planning panel

Carleton Bryant
Staff Attorney
Knox County Sheriff's Office
Knoxville, Tennessee

John Davis
Operations Manager
Colorado Regional Computer Forensics
  Laboratory
Lone Tree, Colorado

Toby Finnie
Director
High Tech Crime Consortium
Tacoma, Washington

Alex Graves
Program Specialist
Federal Law Enforcement Training Center
Brunswick, Georgia

Patrick Hogan
Special Agent
Investigator/DE Examiner
USSS Electronic Crimes Section
Washington, D.C.

Michael J. Menz
HP-IT Security Investigator
Detective
Sacramento High Technology Crimes
  Task Force
Sacramento, California

Sean P. Morgan
White Collar Crime Program Manager
American Prosecutors Research Institute
Alexandria, Virginia

Cynthia Murphy
Detective
Madison Police Department
Madison, Wisconsin

Tom Sadaka
Of Counsel
Berger Singerman
Attorneys at Law
Ft. Lauderdale, Florida

Raemarie Schmidt
Vice President
Digital Intelligence, Inc.
Waukesha, Wisconsin

Todd Shipley
Director, Systems Security and High Tech
  Crime Prevention Training
SEARCH Group, Inc.
Sacramento, California

Chris Stippich
President
Digital Intelligence, Inc.
Waukesha, Wisconsin

Technical Working Group members

Walter E. Bruehs
Forensics Examiner
Forensic Audio, Video and Imaging
  Analysis Unit
Federal Bureau of Investigation
Quantico, Virginia

Tim Dees
Regional Training Coordinator
Oregon Department of Public Safety
  Standards and Training
Kennewick, Washington

Michael W. Finnie
Senior Computer Forensic Specialist
Computer Forensics, Inc.
Seattle, Washington

Carlton Fitzpatrick
Chief, Financial Investigations Branch
Federal Law Enforcement Training Center
U.S. Department of Homeland Security
Glynco, Georgia

Grant Gottfried
MITRE
McLean, Virginia

Ronald J. Green
Senior Vice President
Corporate Information Security
Bank of America
Charlotte, North Carolina

Gerald Griffin
Director
Forensic and Technical Services
U.S. Postal Inspection Service
U.S. Postal Service
Dulles, Virginia

William Harrod
Director, Investigative Response
TruSecure
Herndon, Virginia

Dave Heslep
Sergeant
Maryland State Police
Technical Investigation Division
Columbia, Maryland

Darrell Johnson
Captain
Knox County Sheriff's Office
Knoxville, Tennessee

Kevin Manson
Coordinator
Internet Investigations Training Programs
Financial Fraud Institute
Federal Law Enforcement Training Center
Glynco, Georgia

Michael McCartney
Special Investigator
New York State Attorney General's Office
Buffalo, New York

Bill Moylan
Detective
Nassau County Police Department
Westbury, New York

Thomas Musheno
Forensic Examiner
Forensic Audio, Video and Image Analysis
Federal Bureau of Investigation
Engineering Research Facility
Quantico, Virginia

Tim O'Neill
Hewlett-Packard Information Security
Roseville, California

Scott R. Patronik
Chief, Division of Technology and
 Advancement
Erie County Sheriff's Office
Buffalo, New York

Jim Riccardi, Jr.
Electronic Crime Specialist
CyberScience Lab
National Law Enforcement and
 Corrections Technology Center–Northeast
Rome, New York

Rebecca Richardson
Network Administrator
Montana State University–Billings
Billings, Montana

Alan Roth
Postal Inspector
Forensic and Technical Services
U.S. Postal Service
Dulles, Virginia

Jonathan J. Rusch
Special Counsel for Fraud Prevention
Criminal Division, Fraud Section
U.S. Department of Justice
Washington, D.C.

Kim Schaffer
New Technologies, Inc.
Gresham, Oregon

Michael Schirling
Lieutenant
Burlington Police
Vermont Internet Crimes Task Force
Burlington, Vermont

Greg Schmidt
Computer Forensics
Frisco, Texas

Howard Schmidt
Chief Security Officer
Ebay, Inc.
Campbell, California

Russ Skinner
Sergeant
Maricopa County Sheriff's Office
Computer Crimes Division
Phoenix, Arizona

Fred Smith
Assistant United States Attorney
Albuquerque, New Mexico

Mike Weil
Huron Consulting Group
Chicago, Illinois

Craig Wilson
Detective Sergeant
Kent Police Computer Crime Unit
United Kingdom

Facilitators

Susan Ballou
Program Manager for Forensic Sciences
Office of Law Enforcement Standards
National Institute of Standards and
  Technology
Gaithersburg, Maryland

Anjali R. Swienton
President & CEO
SciLawForensics, Ltd.
Germantown, Maryland

Contents

Chapter 1. Introduction and Investigative Issues

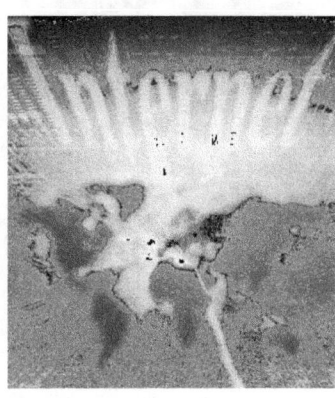

Note: Terms that are defined in the glossary appear in **bold italics** *on their first appearance in the body of the report.*

This report is intended to be a resource for individuals responsible for investigations involving the use of the Internet and other computer networks. It does not encompass a complete discussion of all the issues surrounding the topics in an investigation and does not attempt to provide guidance on traditional investigative procedures.

The use of the Internet and other computer networks has seen explosive growth. As a result, any crime could involve devices that communicate through the Internet or through a network.

The investigator should be aware that criminals may use the Internet for numerous reasons, including—

- Trading/sharing information (e.g., documents, photographs, movies, sound files, text and graphic files, and software programs).

- Concealing their identity.

- Assuming another identity.

- Identifying and gathering information on victims.

- Communicating with co-conspirators.

- Distributing information or misinformation.

- Coordinating meetings, meeting sites, or parcel drops.

Investigations vary in scope and complexity. Evidence of the crime may reside on electronic devices in numerous jurisdictions and may encompass multiple suspects and victims. Complex evidentiary issues are frequently encountered in Internet and network investigations. Sources of information needed to investigate the case may be located anywhere in the world and may not be readily available to the investigator, such as—

- Victims and suspects and their computers.

- Data on workstations/***servers/routers*** of third parties such as businesses, government entities, and educational institutions.

- Internet Service Provider records.

Digital evidence is fragile and can easily be lost. For example:

■ It can change with usage.

■ It can be maliciously and deliberately destroyed or altered.

■ It can be altered due to improper handling and storage.

For these reasons, evidence should be expeditiously retrieved and preserved. Also consider that when investigating offenses involving the Internet, time, date, and time zone information may prove to be very important. Server and computer clocks may not be accurate or set to the local time zone. The investigator should seek other information to confirm the accuracy of time and date stamps.

At the scene, the best judgment of the investigator (based on training, experience, and available resources) will dictate the investigative approach. In some cases a forensic examination of the computer will be needed. The investigator should be aware that any action taken on the computer system might affect the integrity of the evidence. **Only in exigent circumstances** (e.g., imminent threat of loss of life or serious physical injury) should an investigator attempt to gain information directly from a computer on the scene. Any action taken should be well documented.

In some cases it may be sufficient to collect information from the complainant (and computer), document the incident, and forego a forensic examination of the complainant's computer. However, if a suspect's computer is identified and recovered, in most situations it should be submitted for forensic examination to preserve the integrity of the evidence.

Although this special report focuses on the technical portion of these investigations, it is important to remember that a traditional investigative process must be followed: Witnesses must be identified and interviewed, evidence must be collected, investigative processes should be documented, and chain-of-custody and the legal process must be followed. In addition, the investigator should consider the following:

■ Was a crime committed?

■ Who has jurisdiction?

■ What resources are needed to conduct the investigation?

■ Are sufficient resources available to support the investigation?

■ What other resources are available?

■ Are there legal issues for discussion with the prosecutor?

Chapters 2 and 9 provide information that may apply to any Internet or network investigation. The remaining chapters address investigative, technical, and legal issues related to specific types of high-technology crimes.

For further detailed information regarding the preservation and documentation of digital crime scenes, refer to the following National Institute of Justice publications:

Electronic Crime Scene Investigation: A Guide for First Responders (www.ojp.usdoj.gov/nij/pubs-sum/187736.htm).

Forensic Examination of Digital Evidence: A Guide for Law Enforcement (www.ojp.usdoj.gov/nij/pubs-sum/199408.htm).

For further information regarding handling of digital evidence and presenting it effectively in court, refer to:

Digital Evidence in the Courtroom: A Guide for Law Enforcement and Prosecutors (www.ojp.usdoj.gov/nij/pubs-sum/211314.htm).

Chapter 2. Tracing an Internet Address to a Source

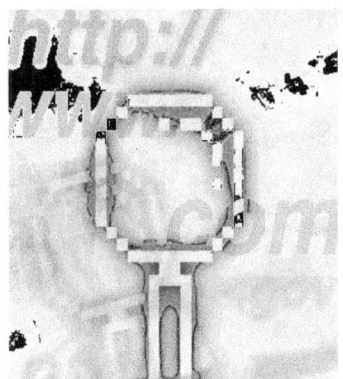

Just as every house has an address, every computer connected to the Internet has an address. This is referred to as an Internet Protocol (IP) address. This chapter explains how IP addresses are assigned and how to trace the addresses to their source.

The investigator may also be presented with other types of addresses. Some examples of these addresses are e-mail addresses and World Wide Web addresses.

Type	Example
E-mail address	someone@nist.gov
Web site address	www.nist.gov
Internet Protocol address	129.6.13.23

All of these may be traced to provide investigative leads. For more information on e-mail and Web site addresses, refer to the specific chapters. Before tracing an IP address, an understanding of the following concepts is useful.

Internet Protocol address

Every device involved in communicating on the Internet requires an IP address.[1] An IP address is a series of four numbers ranging from 0 to 255, separated by periods. The address identifies the specific network and device. An example of an IP address is:

129.6.13.23

A common analogy is to compare an IP address to an apartment address. (See exhibit 1.)

---

[1] For example, devices may be computers, routers, personal digital assistants (PDAs), etc.

Exhibit 1. **IP address and apartment address**

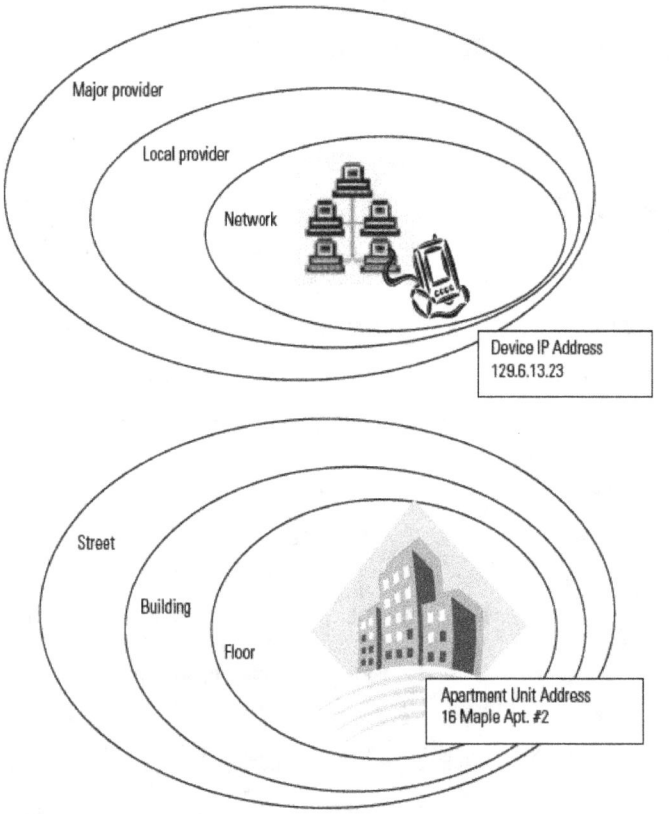

Major provider

Local provider

Network

Device IP Address
129.6.13.23

Street

Building

Floor

Apartment Unit Address
16 Maple Apt. #2

STOP The IP address does not denote a physical location of the device at the time it is connected to the Internet.

IP addressing uses four decimal-separated numbers, which allows for a total of 256^4 or 1,099,511,627,776 unique addresses. This addressing scheme is being expanded to accommodate additional Internet usage. Regardless of the addressing scheme used, the method of tracing the IP address will likely remain the same.

Private IP address

Three groups of IP addresses are specifically reserved for use by any private network and are not seen on the public Internet. Information for these IP addresses comes from the owner of the network. The ranges are:

10.0.0.0	to	10.255.255.255
172.16.0.0	to	172.31.255.255
192.168.0.0	to	192.168.255.255

Internet Service Providers

Internet Service Providers (ISPs) may be commercial vendors or organizations, such as a business or government entity. They may reserve blocks of IP addresses that can be assigned to its users.

ISPs may log the date, time, account user information, and **ANI (Automatic Number Identification)** or caller line identification at the time of connection. If logs are kept, they may be kept for a limited time depending on the established policy of the ISP. Currently, no general legal requirement exists for log preservation; therefore, some ISPs do not store logs. In the event that particular logs are necessary for the investigation, preparing and submitting a preservation letter as described in chapter 9 are important.

Dynamic and static IP addresses

"Dynamic" IP addresses are temporarily assigned from a pool of available addresses registered to an ISP. These addresses are assigned to a device when a user begins an online session. As a result, a device's IP address may vary from one logon session to the next.

"Static" IP addresses are permanently assigned to devices configured to always have the same IP address. A person, business, or organization maintaining a constant Internet presence, such as a Web site, generally requires a static IP address.

Note: The date and time an IP address was assigned must be determined to tie it to a specific device or user account. The ISP may maintain historical log files relating these dynamically assigned IP addresses back to a particular subscriber or user at a particular time.

Packet

Data sent over the Internet are divided into **packets** that are routed through the Internet and reassembled at the destination. When information such as files, e-mail messages, HyperText Markup Language (HTML) documents, or Web pages are sent from one place to another on a network, the network operating system divides the information into chunks of an efficient size for routing. Each of these packets includes the address of the destination. The individual packets for the information being routed may travel different routes through a network. When they have all arrived, they are reassembled into the original file.

Note: Capturing packets is beyond the scope of this special report. However, records of a packet's transmission through a network device may be retained within the logs of that device. It may be necessary to work with the network administrator to obtain these log files.

Network devices and services

Network devices and services include routers,[2] *firewalls,*[3] *proxy servers/gateways,*[4] *Network Address Translation (NAT),*[5] and *Dynamic Host Configuration Protocol (DHCP).*[6] By design, these devices and services may or may not have a logging feature that captures source and destination IP information, login user name, and date and time of logins. Some or all of these network devices and services may alter or mask the true source or destination IP address. It may be necessary to work with the network administrator to determine the true source or destination IP address.

Domain Name System servers

Domain Name System (DNS) servers are the "phonebooks" of the Internet. They maintain directories that match IP addresses with registered domains and resolve the text that people understand (the domain name) into a format that devices understand (the IP address).

In exhibit 2, My PC sends the request for the location of "www.nist.gov." The DNS server responds with the assigned IP address of "129.6.13.23." My PC then requests to display data from IP address 129.6.13.23, the computer on the Internet that hosts the nist.gov Web site.

---

[2] A router is a device that determines the next network point to which a data packet should be forwarded to reach its destination. The router is connected to at least two networks and determines which way to send each data packet based on its current understanding of the state of the networks to which it is connected.

[3] A firewall is a set of related programs that protects the resources of a private network from unauthorized users. A firewall filters all network packets to determine whether to forward them to their destination.

[4] A proxy server/gateway are devices that pass traffic between networks. Typically, a gateway physically sits at the perimeter of an internal network to the Internet. A proxy server may contain cached pages of previously visited Web sites.

[5] Network Address Translation (NAT) is a service that allows computers on a private network to access the Internet by translating a private (reserved) IP address to a public (Internet routable) IP address. NAT modifies outgoing network packets so that the return address is a valid Internet host, thereby protecting the private addresses from public view.

[6] Dynamic Host Configuration Protocol (DHCP) is a service that automates the assignment of IP addresses on a network. DHCP assigns an IP address each time a computer is connected to the network. DHCP uses the concept of a "lease" or amount of time that a given IP address will be valid for a specific computer. DHCP can dynamically reassign IP addresses for networks that have a requirement for more IP addresses than are available.

Exhibit 2. **Domain Name System (DNS)**

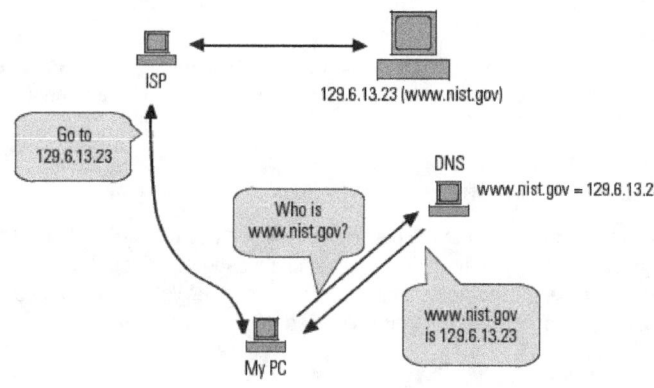

Registering domain names

A person or an organization can register a domain name as long as it is not already regis-tered. Domain names are registered with the Internet Corporation for Assigned Names and Numbers (ICANN), a nonprofit organization responsible for Internet address assign-ment and domain name server management.

Information required to register a domain name includes name, address, phone number, billing information, e-mail address, and technical and administrative contact information. In addition to this information, the date that a domain was registered may be available from the registrar. Although this information may provide investigative leads, the investi-gator should be aware that the information originates from the person registering the domain name and may be fictitious.

Spoofing, masking, and redirecting

Advanced methods of obscuring actions on the Internet include hiding the IP address, pretending to be someone else, and sending traffic through another IP address. These methods are commonly referred to as masking,[7] spoofing,[8] and redirecting.[9] Advanced training is required to investigate or identify when these actions have taken place. Therefore, even after completing legal process, traditional investigative methods may still be necessary to identify the end user. In some cases, masking, spoofing, or redirecting may prevent the identification of the user.

---

[7] IP masking is a method of hiding or obscuring the true source IP address.

[8] IP spoofing is a method of impersonating another system's IP address.

[9] IP redirecting is a method of forwarding or routing Internet traffic to an obscured IP address.

Tracing an IP address or domain name

Scenario

A citizen makes a claim that while surfing the Internet, he came across a Web site that he believes should be looked at by law enforcement. The citizen provides the Web site name of www.nist.gov.

Step 1. Resolve domain name

The first step is to resolve the domain name of www.nist.gov to an IP address. Many commercial software tools are available to assist an investigator in resolving domain names into IP addresses. In addition, many publicly available Web sites will resolve domain names. Some of the more commonly used Web sites include the following:

www.network-tools.com
www.samspade.org
www.geektools.com
www.dnsstuff.com

Note: The above sites contain more than one tool.

The features and level of detail available from the above sites may differ. The common utilities on these Web sites include the following:

whois	A utility that queries a database that includes domain names, IP addresses, and points of contact, including names, postal addresses, and telephone numbers.
nslookup	A utility that queries a domain name server for a particular name and provides the IP addresses for a particular domain. Caution: The IP addresses may not be returned from a validated source and therefore could be erroneous.
traceroute	A utility that attempts to trace the path a packet takes as it travels from one device to another. Traceroute can help to narrow down the geographic location of a particular device.

Note: Investigators should be aware that inquiries made on these sites might be monitored and recorded. It is important to conduct sensitive inquiries from a computer that is not traceable back to the investigating agency.

Step 2. Determine and record domain name registration

The next step is to determine and record the domain name registration information. The following online resources can be used to obtain registration information:

www.network-tools.com
www.samspade.org
www.geektools.com
www.apnic.net (Asia)
www.checkdomain.com
www.lacnic.net
www.ripe.net (Europe)
www.whois.com
www.dnsstuff.com

Exhibit 3. Domain name registration

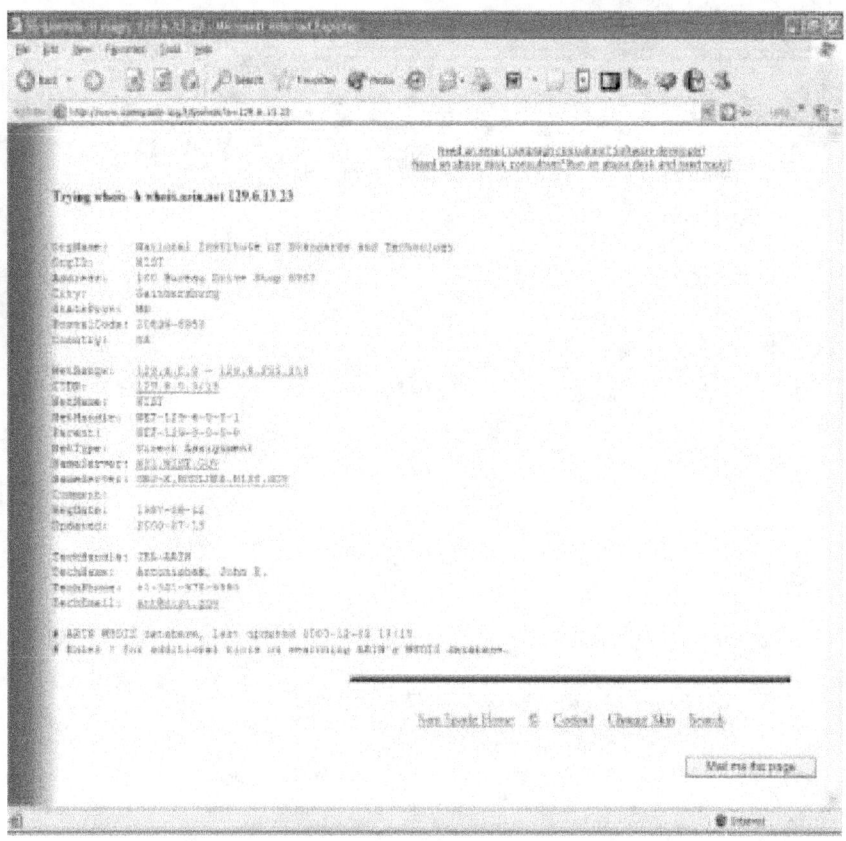

Exhibit 3 shows the registration information for www.nist.gov and has resolved it to the IP address 129.6.13.23. The typical information provided includes—

■ Registered owner's name and address.

■ Billing information.

■ Administrative contact.

■ Range of IP addresses associated with the domain.

■ Technical contact information.

The listed contacts may provide additional information about the specific computer being sought, including its location and the person designated to receive legal process.

Note: The same process can be used to resolve an IP address to a domain name to obtain contact information.

Where's the evidence?

Information can be found in numerous locations, including—

- User's computer.

- ISP for the user.

- ISP for a victim and/or suspect.

- Log files contained on the victim's and/or suspect's—

  — Routers.

  — Firewalls.

  — Web servers.

  — E-mail servers.

  — Other connected devices.

See exhibit 4 for a graphic representation of the information flow.

Given an IP address and a date and time (including the time zone), most ISPs can identify the registered user assigned to the IP address at the specific time, enabling the investigator to request additional information. However, the investigator may need to use traditional investigative methods to identify the person using the account at that time.

Step 3. Provide legal service of process

The third step is to determine the appropriate parties to contact and/or serve legal process, depending on the facts of the investigation as discussed in subsequent chapters. Warrants, court orders, or subpoenas are typically required to release exact end-user information to law enforcement. Many of these requirements are governed by the Electronic Communications Privacy Act (ECPA) and other applicable Federal and State laws. A preservation letter may assist in preserving information until proper legal requirements can be met. These requests should specify the IP address and the date and time, including the time zone. Be cognizant of the need for expeditious service of preservation letters under 18 USC § 2703(f) (appendix G). See chapter 9 for more details on legal requirements and appendix H for sample language.

Information that may be obtained from the ISP includes—

- **Subscriber information** such as the registered owner, address, and payment method.

- **Transactional information** such as connection times, dates, and IP address used.

Exhibit 4. Where to find information

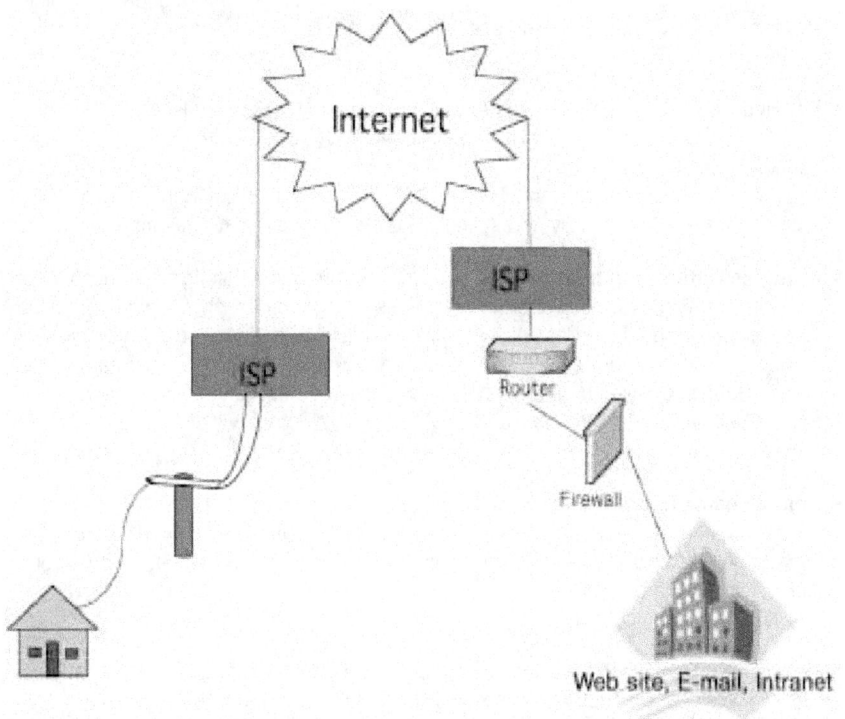

■ **Content** such as e-mail messages, data files, and stored programs.

Some of the information used in tracing an IP address or end user may be obtained from ISPs or network administrators. This information typically includes account information, e-mail address information, IP address, and domain name. It may or may not contain information about the owner or user. Based on the information received, additional investigation may be required. Additional subpoenas, search warrants, court orders, and preservation letters may need to be served on entities identified by the previous legal process. For example, if the original IP address resolves to "BIG-ISP.com," legal process is issued to BIG-ISP.com to identify the user of a particular IP address at a particular date and time. The return identifies "Medium-ISP.com" as the user of that IP address. (A common practice among smaller ISPs is to lease blocks of IP addresses from larger ISPs.) At this point, additional legal process must be issued to "Medium-ISP.com." This process continues until the information identifies the user logged in on that particular IP address for a specific date and time or until all investigative leads are exhausted.

Sample language. When drafting legal process, the following sample language may be useful. However, the ISP may require other specific language.

- **ISP account information:** "Any and all subscriber information relating to the account of (Name) including but not limited to user identity, user account information, screen names, account status, detailed billing records, e-mail account information, caller line identification (ANI), account maintenance history notes, and IP history from (Date) to present."

- **E-mail address information:** "Any and all subscriber information relating to the individual who registered and maintains the e-mail address of (JonDoe@Email.com) including but not limited to user identity, user account information, screen names, account status, detailed billing records, e-mail account information, caller line identification (ANI), account maintenance history notes, and IP history from (Date) to present."

- **IP address information:** "Any and all subscriber information relating to the account of the individual who was assigned the IP address of (IP Address) on (Date) at (Time and Time Zone) and the IP address of (IP Address) for (Date) at (Date and Time Zone) including but not limited to user identity, user account information, screen names, account status, detailed billing records, e-mail account information, caller line identification (ANI), account maintenance history notes, and IP history from (Date) to present."

- **Domain name information:** "Any and all information relating to the identity of the individual who registered and maintains the domain names of (www.xxxxxxxx.com) and (www.xxxxxxxx.org) including but not limited to all account information, billing records including credit card number or other payment information, user identity, IP history, and caller line identification."

- **Web page information:** "All information on the individual who created and maintains the (ISP) Web page (Web page name) including but not limited to user identity, user account information, billing records, e-mail account information, caller line identification, usage logs, and IP history."

- **Telnet session providers:** "Any and all IP history relating to Internet traffic of (xxxxx.net) and user logs of (xxxx.net's) *Telnet* sessions for (Date) and (Date) including but not limited to user identity, user name, user commands issued, and user address."

- **Point of Presence (POP) information:** "Any and all information relating to the (ANS.NET or other ISP) *Point of Presence* location that issued the IP (IP Address) on (Date/Time) including but not limited to dial-in access phone number, physical address, and (Telephone Company) to whom the dial-in access phone number is subscribed."

- **Outgoing telephone records:** "Any and all information including but not limited to subscriber information and billing information for the address of (Address of Subscriber). Any and all information including, but not limited to subscriber information and billing information for the telephone number of (Telephone Number). Include a listing of any local outgoing calls made from the above address. Include above information for any and all telephone numbers listed for the above address for the period of (Date/Time)."

Summary

All communications on the Internet and across networks rely on an IP address to reach their destination. The key to investigating crimes relating to the Internet and networks is to identify the originating IP address and trace it to a source. These skills enable an investigator to locate additional sources of evidence, corroborate victim and witness statements, and potentially locate a suspect.

Chapter 3. Investigations Involving E-Mail

E-mail can be a starting point or a key element in many investigations. E-mail is the electronic equivalent of a letter or a memo and may include attachments or enclosures. Like paper or postal mail, an e-mail may represent evidence in many types of investigations. No longer exclusive to desktop computers, e-mail is now readily exchanged using many portable devices such as cell phones, personal digital assistants (PDAs), and pagers.

How e-mail works

E-mail can be generated by different devices and methods but, most commonly, a user composes the message on her own computer and then sends it off to her mail server. At this point the user's computer is finished with the job, but the mail server still has to deliver the message. A mail server is like an electronic post office—it sends and receives electronic mail. Most of the time, the mail server is separate from the computer where the mail was composed. (See exhibit 5.)

Exhibit 5. **Generating e-mail**

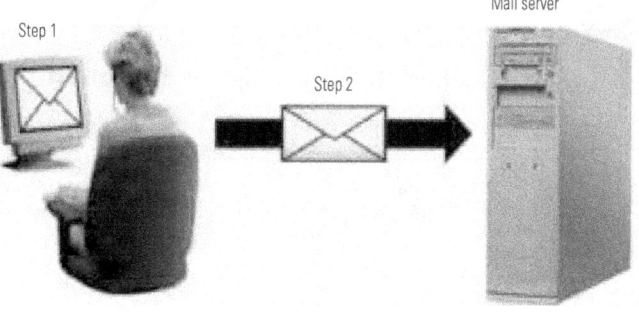

The sender's mail server delivers the message by finding the recipient's mail server and forwards the message to that location. The message then resides on that second mail server and is available to the recipient. The software program being used to compose and read the e-mail message is sometimes referred to as the e-mail **client**. Depending on how the recipient's e-mail client is configured, a copy of the message could be found on the recipient's computer, another electronic device such as an all-in-one telephone or

Exhibit 6. **Delivering e-mail**

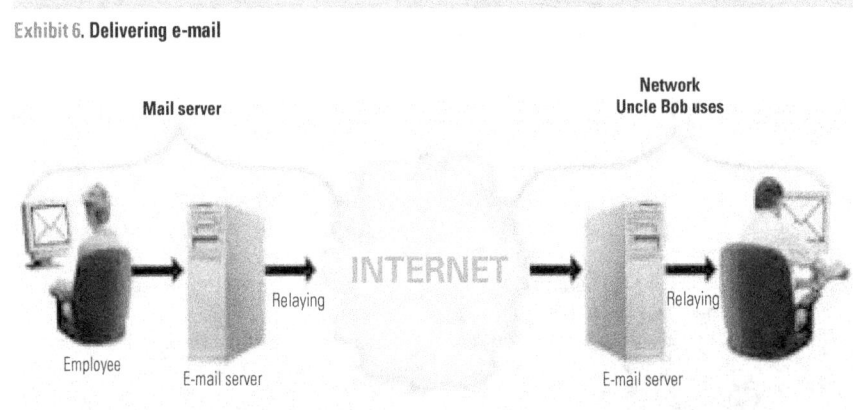

PDA, and/or the mail server or its backup tapes. A copy of the message may also be found on the sender's computer (in the "sent" box or trash), or on the sender's mail server or its backup tapes. (See exhibit 6.)

As the message travels through the communications network, an abbreviated record of the e-mail's journey is recorded in an area of the message called the ***header.*** As the message is routed through one or more mail servers, each server adds its own information to the message header. **The investigator may be able to identify Internet Protocol (IP) addresses from the header and use this information to determine the sender of the message using techniques discussed in chapter 2.**

Basic components of an e-mail

Various methods are used for creating and sending an e-mail message. The appearance of an e-mail message depends on the device or software program used. However, a message typically has a header and a body and may also have attachments. The e-mail header contains addressing information and the route that an e-mail takes from sender to receiver. The body contains the content of the communication. Attachments may be any type of file such as pictures, documents, sound, and video.

When initially viewing an e-mail message, only a small portion of the e-mail header may be displayed. This usually is information put into the message by the sender, as represented in exhibit 7.

Exhibit 7. E-mail components

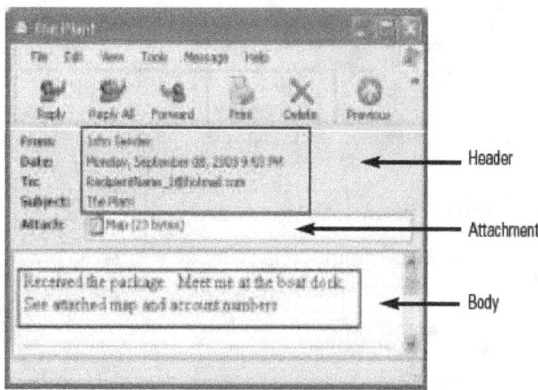

However, the e-mail message depicted in exhibit 7 does not display all of the available information. Additional information associated with the e-mail may be obtained by looking at the header in more detail, which can be done in different ways depending on the software program being used. See appendix C for instructions on how to reveal detailed header information for common e-mail clients. Be aware that not all e-mail clients are listed, and updates to the clients may change the method of obtaining the detailed header information.

The journey of the message can usually be reconstructed by reading the e-mail header from bottom to top. As the message passes through additional mail servers, the mail server will add its information above the previous information in the header. **One of the most important pieces of information for the investigator to obtain from the detailed header is the originating IP address.** In the example in exhibit 8, the originating IP address is [165.247.94.223]

Exhibit 8. E-mail header

```
12.  X-Message-Info: JGTYoYF78jEv6iDU7aTDV/xX2xdjzKcH
11.  Received: from web11603.mail.yahoo.com ([216.136.172.55]) by mc4-
     f4 with Microsoft SMTPSVC(5.0.2195.5600);
              Mon, 8 Sep 2003 18:53:07 -0700
10.  Message-ID: 20030909015303.27404.qmail@web11603.mail.yahoo.com
 9.  Received: from [165.247.94.223] by web11603.mail.yahoo.com via
     HTTP; Mon, 08 Sep 2003 18:53:03 PDT
 8.  Date: Mon, 8 Sep 2003 18:53:03 -0700 (PDT)
 7.  From: John Sender <sendersname2003@yahoo.com>
 6.  Subject: The Plan!
 5.  To: RecipientName_1@hotmail.com
 4.  MIME-Version: 1.0
     Content-Type: multipart/mixed; boundary="0-2041413029-
     1063072383=:26811"
 3.  Return-Path: sendersname2003@yahoo.com
 2.  X-OriginalArrivalTime: 09 Sep 2003 01:53:07.0873 (UTC)
     FILETIME=[1DBDB910:01C37675]

 1.  --0-2041413029-1063072383=:26811
     Content-Type: multipart/alternative; boundary="0-871459572-
     1063072383=:26811"

     --0-871459572-1063072383=:26811
     Content-Type: text/plain; charset=us-ascii

     Received the package. Meet me at the boat dock.
     See attached map and account numbers
```

To understand the parts of the e-mail header in exhibit 8, the header is reproduced below with a line-by-line description. Note that the e-mail header is composed of two general areas, the *envelope header* and the *message header*.

The *envelope header* contains information added to the header by the mail servers that receive the message during the journey. The "Received:" lines and the Message-ID line are the main components of the envelope header and are generally more difficult to **spoof**. In the following example, lines 9 through 12 are part of the envelope header.

The *message header* contains information added to the header by the user's e-mail client. This is generally user-created information and is the easiest to spoof. It contains the To:, From:, Return-Path:, Subject:, Content-Type:, and the first Date and time. In the following example, lines 2 though 8 are part of the message header.

12. X-Message-Info: JGTYoYF78jEv6iDU7aTDV/xX2xdjzKcH

X-headers are nonstandard headers and are not essential for the delivery of mail. The usefulness of the X-header needs to be explored with the Internet Service Provider (ISP).

11. **Received: from web11603.mail.yahoo.com ([216.136.172.55]) by mc4-f4 with Microsoft SMTPSVC(5.0.2195.5600);**
    Mon, 8 Sep 2003 18:53:07 -0700

Received:

*This "Received" line is the last stamp that was placed in the header. It is placed there by the last mail server to receive the message and will identify the mail server from which it was received. Note that the date and time stamp is generated by the receiving mail server and indicates its offset from **UTC** (-0700). In this example, the mail server's name is indicated. This can be accomplished by either the receiving server resolving the IP address of the last mail server or the prior mail server broadcasting its name.*

10. **Message-ID: 20030909015303.27404.qmail@web11603.mail.yahoo.com**

Message-ID:

A unique identifier assigned to each message. It is usually assigned by the first e-mail server and is a key piece of information for the investigator. Unlike the originating IP address (below), which can give subscriber information, the message-id can link the message to the sender if appropriate logs are kept.

9. **Received: from [165.247.94.223] by web11603.mail.yahoo.com via HTTP; Mon, 08 Sep 2003 18:53:03 PDT**

Received:

The bottom "Received" line identifies the IP address of the originating mail server. It could indicate the name of the server, the protocol used, and the date and time settings of the server. Note the time zone information that is reported.

CAUTION: If the date and time associated with the e-mail are important to the investigation, consider that this "Received" time recorded in the e-mail header comes from the e-mail server and may not be accurate.

8. **Date: Mon, 8 Sep 2003 18:53:03 -0700 (PDT)**

Date:

This date is assigned by the sender's machine and it may not agree with the e-mail server's date and time stamp. If the creation date and time of the e-mail are important to the investigation, consider that the time recorded in the e-mail header comes from the sender's machine and may not be accurate.

7. **From: John Sender <sendersname2003@yahoo.com>**

From:

This is information usually configured in the e-mail client by the user and may not be reliable.

6. **Subject: The Plan!**

> Subject:

This is information entered by the user.

5. **To: RecipientName_1@hotmail.com**

> To:

This is information entered by the user.

4. **MIME-Version: 1.0**
   Content-Type: multipart/mixed; boundary="0-2041413029-1063072383=:26811"

The purpose of these two lines is to give the recipient's e-mail client information on how to interpret the content of the message.

3. **Return-Path: sendersname2003@yahoo.com**

> Return-Path:

This is information usually configured in the e-mail client by the user and may not be reliable.

2. **X-OriginalArrivalTime: 09 Sep 2003 01:53:07.0873 (UTC)**
   FILETIME=[1DBDB910:01C37675]

X-headers are nonstandard headers and are not essential for the delivery of mail. The usefulness of the X-header needs to be explored with the Provider ISP.

1. **--0-2041413029-1063072383=:26811**

E-mail client information; not relevant to the investigation.

Once the IP addresses are identified in the header, the procedures outlined in chapter 2 can be used to trace the journey of the e-mail. Be aware that IP addresses can be created or spoofed in an attempt to hide the true identity of the sender.

Time stamping

Investigators should be aware that when examining e-mail headers, times may not be consistent. Date and time stamps related to the header should be scrutinized as these times may be added by different servers in different parts of the world and different time zones and may not be consistent. In addition, clocks built into computer systems and powered by batteries—especially those on personal computers—may not always be accurately set or may not keep time correctly, resulting in the wrong time. Special consideration should be given to looking for time zone information related to the time.

Exhibit 9 shows a chronological sequence of actions with different clock times involved in transmitting e-mail.

Exhibit 9. E-mail time sequence

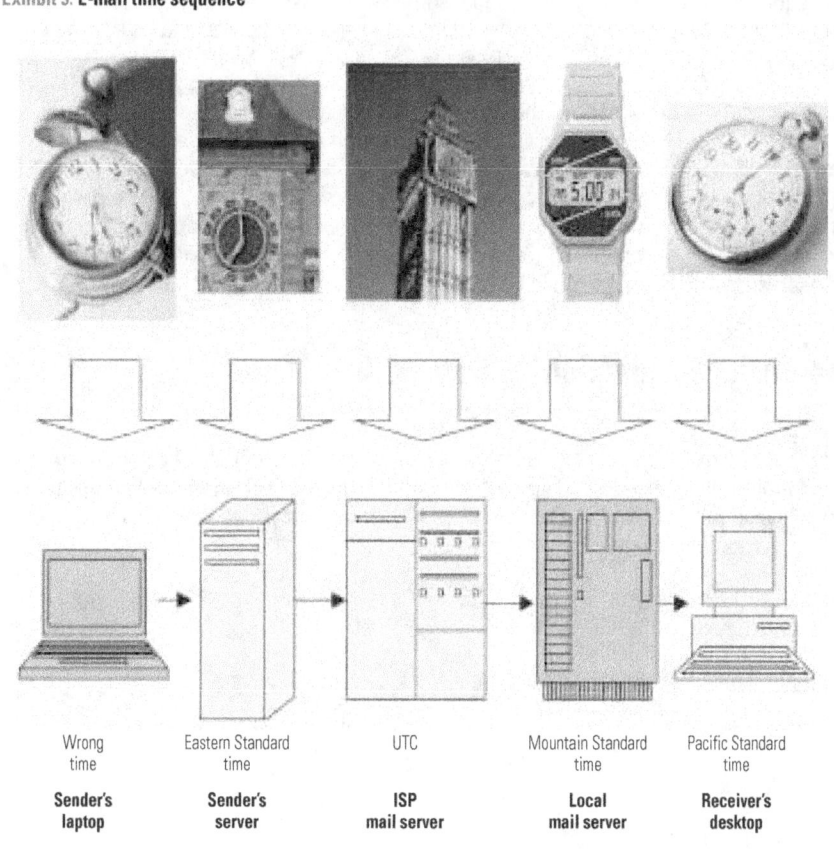

Wrong time	Eastern Standard time	UTC	Mountain Standard time	Pacific Standard time
Sender's laptop	**Sender's server**	**ISP mail server**	**Local mail server**	**Receiver's desktop**

Issues to be aware of

Spoofed e-mail headers. Anything up to the last (topmost) "Received:" line in the message header can be spoofed, or faked. Compare the information in the message header with that in the envelope header. If the two do not agree, the possibility exists that the e-mail may have been spoofed.

Anonymizers. Anonymizers are e-mail servers that strip identifying information from the message before forwarding it. Although valid reasons exist for using an anonymizer service, many individuals use the service to conceal their identity. If an anonymizer is used, the investigator may not be able to trace the e-mail to its origin as logs are frequently not maintained by these services.

Remote locations. Note that many public places exist where Internet access is available, such as libraries, schools, airports, hotels, and Internet cafes. If an e-mail message is sent from one of these locations, determining the actual sender may be difficult.

Delayed send. Many providers and e-mail clients have the ability to allow the sender to schedule the time an e-mail is sent. Also, some servers send e-mail at a certain prescheduled time. Either of these situations could allow an individual to be at another location at the time the mail is actually sent.

E-mail location. Regardless of the type of e-mail being used, the message can be stored in multiple locations. Consider obtaining it from as many sources as possible. For example, if the message is Web based and stored by a service provider (e.g., Hotmail®, Yahoo!®), time is of the essence as many of these companies have a policy to purge information after a certain period of time. A preservation letter issued to the provider would be a necessary measure to prevent purging of data. Further information about preservation orders can be found in chapter 9.

Forensic examination

STOP An investigator should not attempt to examine a computer system if the investigator has not received special training in forensic examination of computers. The investigator should follow agency policy or contact an agency with a forensic examination capability.

A forensic investigation of a computer system might reveal additional information, such as—

- Other e-mail messages related to the investigation.

- Other e-mail addresses.

- Sender information.

- Content of the communications.

- IP addresses.

- Date and time information.

- User information.

- Attachments.

- Passwords.

- Application logs that show evidence of spoofing.

Legal considerations

As in all investigations involving computer evidence and the recovery of computer data, specific legal requirements and reliable forensic procedures must be followed to obtain admissible evidence and to avoid civil and criminal liability. See chapter 9 for further information and consult with legal counsel when appropriate.

In determining the legal issues for the investigation, at a minimum the following should be considered:

- The Fourth Amendment.

- Electronic Communications Privacy Act (18 U.S.C. § 2501 *et seq.*).

- Electronic Communications Privacy Act (18 U.S.C. § 2701 *et seq.*). (This section is referred to as Stored Wire and Electronic Communications Section.)

- Pen Register and Trap and Trace Statute (18 U.S.C. § 3121 *et seq.*).

- Title III Wiretaps.

- Applicable State laws.

The Fourth Amendment

If the e-mail resides on the sender's or recipient's computer or other device, then the steps taken to secure that evidence must be analyzed under the Fourth Amendment and State constitutional requirements. The investigator must consider whether the person on whose computer the evidence resides has a reasonable expectation of privacy on that computer. The Fourth Amendment would require a search warrant or one of the recognized exceptions to the search warrant requirements such as consent or exigent circumstances.

Electronic Communications Privacy Act

If the e-mail is stored by an Internet Service Provider or any other communications network, retrieval of that evidence must be analyzed under the Electronic Communications Privacy Act (ECPA). ECPA creates statutory restrictions on government access to such evidence from ISPs or other electronic communications service providers.

ECPA requires different legal processes to obtain specific types of information. Basic subscriber information (name, address, billing information including a credit card number, telephone toll billing records, subscriber's telephone number, type of service, and length of service) can be obtained by subpoena, court order, or search warrant. Transactional information (such as Web sites visited, e-mail addresses of others from whom or to whom the subscriber exchanged e-mail, and buddy lists) can be obtained by court order or search warrant. A search warrant can be used to obtain content information from retrieved e-mail and must be used to obtain unretrieved stored e-mails.[10] Real-time access (traffic intercepted as it is sent or received) requires a wiretap order under the provisions of Title III. For further details refer to chapter 9.

---

[10] For investigating agencies located within the Ninth Circuit (California, Oregon, Washington, Arizona, Montana, Idaho, Nevada, Alaska, Hawaii, Guam, and the Northern Mariana Islands), a search warrant must be used to obtain content information from any e-mail, as discussed in more detail in chapter 9.

Pen Register and Trap and Trace Statute

This applies not only to telephone communications, but also Internet communications. For example, every e-mail communication contains to and from information. A pen/trap device captures noncontent information of communications in real time.

Title III wiretaps

Title III may need to be considered, depending on how an ISP executes a request to obtain a subscriber's e-mail. However, to obtain e-mail in real time as it is ingoing and outgoing from the ISP, a Title III wiretap order is always required.

Summary

Information obtained from an e-mail message can be valuable evidence. This chapter provides techniques to obtain one piece of the investigation puzzle. Once the e-mail account subscriber is identified, however, other investigative techniques should be used to actually place an individual at the keyboard at the time the message was sent. Keep in mind the legal procedures that must be followed to ensure the evidence gathered can be used in court.

Chapter 4. Investigations Involving Web Sites

This chapter provides guidance regarding methods and practices to conduct Web site investigations. The investigator should be aware that access to a Web site may be monitored by the target of the investigation. Monitoring may reveal the investigator's identity, thus compromising the investigation. Use of an undercover computer and Internet Service Provider (ISP) account or other covert methods should be considered.

STOP Investigations should not be conducted using the suspect's or victim's computer unless exigent circumstances exist, as the integrity of the evidence may be affected.

Generally, a Web site is a collection of related Web pages or files (such as pictures, sounds, or text) that is stored on a Web server. The typical language that these pages are written in is HyperText Markup Language (HTML). This language allows users to easily navigate between related pages or files in the collection. It also allows a related collection of pages to be linked to another related collection of pages. Simply put, HTML allows links between Web sites.

A Web server is a computer with special software that provides Web pages to clients across the Internet or an intranet. A Web server can host multiple Web sites, many of which may not be related to the ongoing investigation. Additionally, the files that comprise a single Web site may exist on more than one Web server.

A Web page is accessed by typing a Uniform Resource Locator (URL) into a Web browser such as Internet Explorer®, Netscape® Navigator, or Mozilla. The URL is the address of a resource, or file, available on the Internet. The URL contains the *protocol* of the resource (e.g., http://, https://), the domain name for the resource, and the hierarchical name for the file (address). For example, a page on the Internet may be at the URL http://www.nist.gov. The beginning part, http://, provides the protocol, the next part, www, is a pointer to a Web server, and nist.gov is the domain. See chapter 2 for more information on domain names and the IP addresses associated with them.

Hyperlinks (links) are shortcuts that allow users to navigate from one Web page to another Web page or file without manually entering the full URL address. Links may be hidden on the Web pages so that only users who know where to look will likely find the links. Links may also automatically redirect the Web browser to a different Web site.

Investigators should be aware that although Web pages are typically written in HTML, they may also be written in "scripting" languages. These languages allow the Web page to display individualized content for each user. The content may be tailored to each user's

Internet Protocol (IP) address, previously visited Web sites, stored cookies, or other criteria. Therefore, it is possible for two people who simultaneously navigate to the same URL to view different content.

Viewing the HTML source of a Web page

The HTML source of a Web page is text that defines the content and format of a page. In addition to the graphical representation provided to the viewer, the page may contain additional information related to its author, programming code, metadata,[11] and other identifying information that may not be displayed in Web page view. Most common Web browsers allow users to view the source of a Web page. Exhibit 10 shows a screen capture for the www.nist.gov Web site, followed by the HTML source information. To view the HTML source using Internet Explorer®, select "view" on the toolbar, then select "source" on the drop-down menu.

Note: Techniques are available that can obscure the HTML source while still allowing normal viewing of the Web page in a browser.

Capturing Web page data

Depending on the nature and scope of the investigation, capturing the information from a single Web page or the entire contents of a Web site may be useful. The techniques for obtaining this information may include screen captures, the "save as" command, Web site capture tools, or locating and seizing the Web server.

Screen capture

Several methods are available for capturing a screen shot of a Web page. One method is a Windows® function [Ctrl]+[PrntScrn], which will capture the entire screen by copying it to the Windows® *clipboard.* The image may then be pasted ([Ctrl]+[v] or Edit > Paste) into another application, such as a word-processing program or graphics editor, for preservation. Another method is to use a third-party software application specifically designed to capture images of screens or active windows. These methods may only capture the displayed content of the active window and may not capture content that is outside the display of the active window. The HTML source will not be captured unless it is displayed.

"Save as" command

A simple method to capture Web page information that may include the HTML source and embedded files is to use the "save as" command within the Web browser. This command will save the Web page to a specified location on the computer the investigator is using. In exhibit 11, the "save as" command is shown on the left, and the destination of the Web page capture is shown on the right. Note that depending on the version of the

---

[11] Metadata in this context is information that describes the attributes or search keywords that have been embedded in a Web page's source code.

Exhibit 10. Screen capture and HTML source for NIST Web site

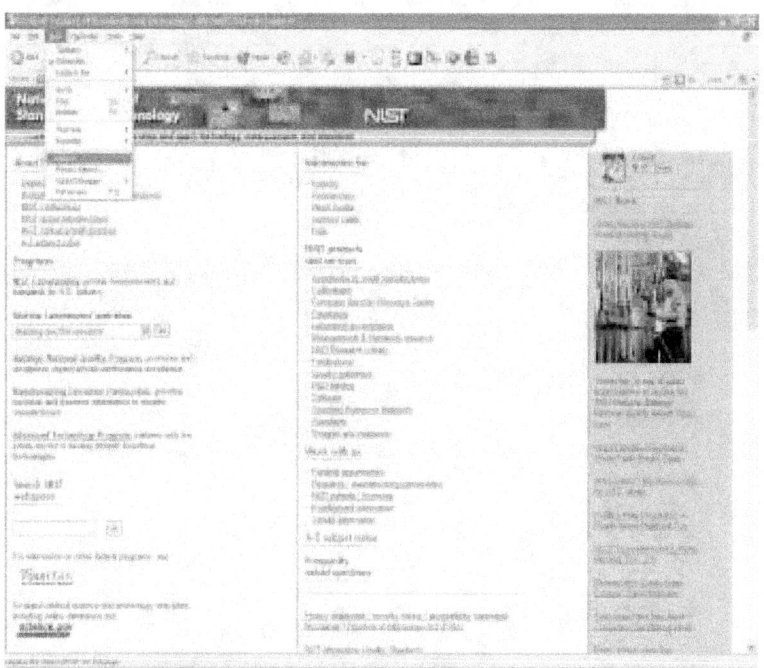

Web browser used, several "Save as type" options may be used to capture the complete page and all of its embedded files. In exhibit 11, the "Save as type" option will result in the entire Web page with all of the embedded files being saved to a folder located in the same directory. A good practice is to test and verify the information that is captured using the different "save as" options before using this technique in an investigation. Once the capture is completed, it should be immediately verified to ensure that all of the information sought has been saved.

Exhibit 11. Save as command and Web page capture

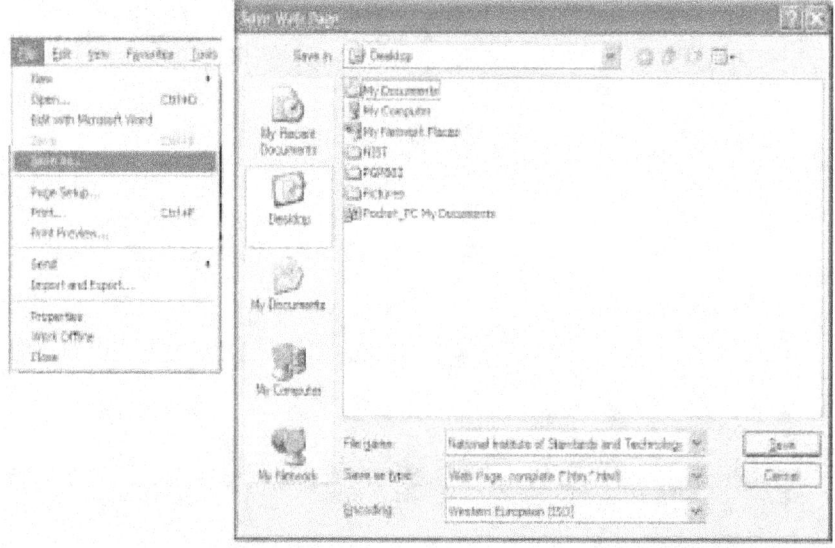

Web site capture tools

A way to automate the capture of a collection of pages within a Web site is through the use of third-party applications. It would be time consuming to manually navigate to and save each Web page on a large Web site. Numerous commercial and freeware tools are available for capturing Web sites. The use of specific tools is beyond the scope of this document. In general these programs are designed to navigate to each link on a Web page and capture all of the content, including embedded files and source code, of those links.

It is important for the investigator to be aware that the content of the current Web site may have changed since the initiation of the investigation. Therefore, the date and time of Web site captures should be documented. Determining previous content of many Web sites may be possible through the use of Web archiving sites (e.g., the *Wayback*

Machine searching tool, http://www.archive.org) or similar sites. For details on how these sites work, visit and read the site documentation.

Note: For Web sites written in scripting languages, it may not be possible to capture all the specific content of interest with Web site capture tools.

Locating and seizing the Web server

In some investigations in which a Web site is being used to perpetrate a crime (e.g., distribution of child pornography), locating and seizing the Web server should be considered. The Web server may contain the content and HTML source, as well as transactional logs that show the IP addresses of users who connect to and download from the Web site. The server may also store user names, passwords, payment methods, and other pertinent investigative information. To locate and identify a Web server, it will be necessary to obtain the IP address and other identifying information and to establish the requisite legal basis to seize and search the Web server. See chapter 2 for details on how to determine the IP address for Web sites by domain.

STOP Personal civil liability issues may be associated with the seizure of Web sites co-hosted on the Web server that are unrelated to the investigation.

Legal issues

Investigations involving Web sites may be governed by the Electronic Communications Privacy Act (ECPA), the Fourth Amendment, and the Privacy Protection Act. Refer to chapter 9 for discussion of these legal issues.

Summary

In the course of an investigation, the investigator may need to determine and preserve the contents of a Web site. Preserving this information may be as simple as capturing a screen shot of the relevant material, but techniques to capture the underlying HTML source and the entire contents of a Web page are also explained. The investigator should be aware that Web page content is dynamic and can change often. This chapter provides a potential resource for viewing the historical content of a Web page.

Chapter 5. Investigations Involving Instant Message Services, Chat Rooms, and IRC

This chapter is intended to be a resource for an investigation involving the use of instant messengers (IM), chat rooms, or Internet Relay Chat (IRC). It does not encompass a complete discussion of all the issues surrounding the use of these communications in an investigation and additional expertise may be needed for a more detailed investigation.

IM, chat rooms, and IRC allow users to communicate with each other in real time. No longer exclusive to desktop computers, instant messaging, chat, and IRC are now readily exchanged using many portable devices such as cell phones, personal digital assistants (PDAs), pagers, and other communication devices. In this chapter, the term "computer" refers collectively to all such devices. Online messenger programs, chat rooms, and IRC frequently allow voice, video, and file exchange as well. The voice and video material can be prerecorded or transmitted live. Most chat rooms and IRC have multiple participants, while instant messengers allow computer users to communicate directly one to one. During a chat or IRC session, the ability to send and receive private messages may also be available.

Instant message services

Numerous software programs and services are available that enable users to communicate in real time. They perform similar functions, but vary in features and the information that is retained on the computer system. Some examples include—

- America Online (AOL®)

- AOL Instant Messenger™ (AIM)

- ICQ

- IRC

- MSN Messenger

- Net Meeting

- Trillian

- Yahoo!® Messenger

- Windows® Messenger

Prior to using an instant message service or chat room, most services require the user to provide or create an e-mail account, as in the example in exhibit 12. Some companies, such as Yahoo!® and Hotmail®, provide free e-mail accounts. In many cases, the information provided is not verified and may not be accurate. As a result, users of these accounts can easily conceal their identities and personal information.

Exhibit 12. **E-mail account creation (from Hotmail®)**

How IM services work

A user must first establish an account and create a screen name or nickname. The user information provided when creating the account may be falsified. However, some message services log the Internet Protocol (IP) address that was in use at the time the account was created. This information may be obtained from the message service provider with appropriate legal process. See chapter 2 for a discussion of tracing an IP address and the usefulness of the information obtained.

Once an account has been established, a user has a number of options available to find other individuals to communicate with online. People can initiate contact through disclosing their screen names or can search for others by characteristics described in user profiles. Exhibit 13 shows a contact list.

Exhibit 13. Contact list

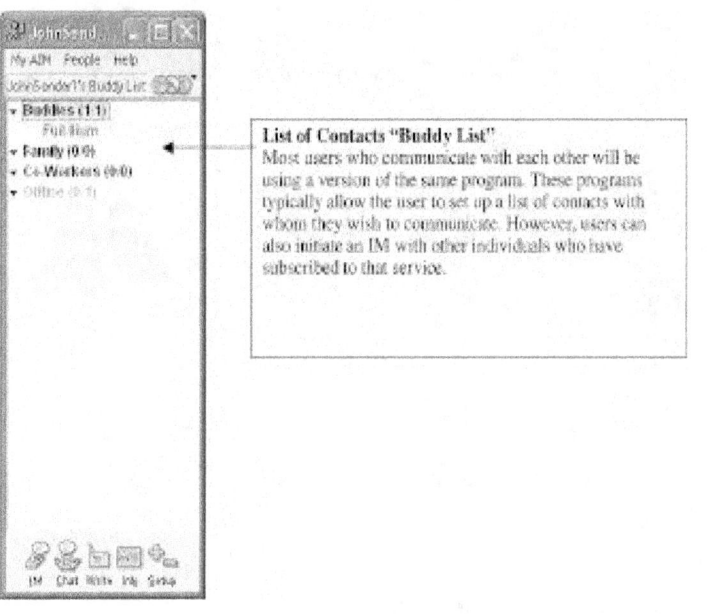

A user initiates a communication by opening the IM program, selecting the user name that he wants to communicate with, typing in the message, and clicking a "send" button. If the other user is online, the text will appear, almost instantly, in a window on the recipient's display. While the session is active, the complete text of the conversation may appear in both windows, but the windows may have to be scrolled in order to view the entire message. The communication appears to the users as being "point-to-point" (computer to computer) even though it may have multiple relay points during its travel. (See exhibit 14 for an instant messaging sample.)

Exhibit 14. **Instant messaging**

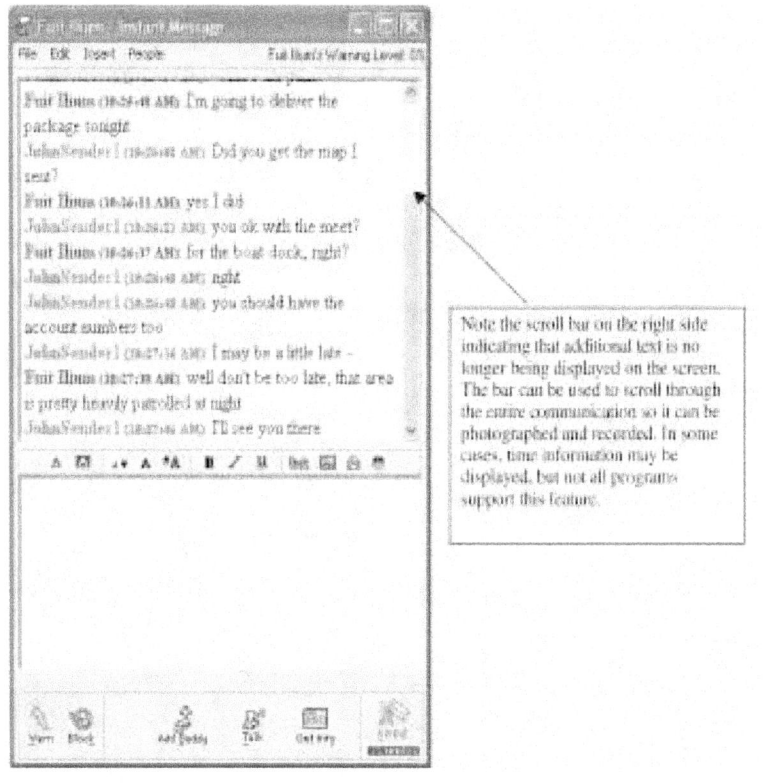

Note the scroll bar on the right side indicating that additional text is no longer being displayed on the screen. The bar can be used to scroll through the entire communication so it can be photographed and recorded. In some cases, time information may be displayed, but not all programs support this feature.

Investigative considerations

For IM-related complaints, obtaining the following information from the complainant may be beneficial.

■ The computer being used to receive the communication.

■ The screen or user name (victim and suspect).

■ The owner of the Internet Service Provider (ISP) account being used.

■ The IM service being used and version of the software.

■ The content (witness account of contact or activity).

■ The date and time the message was received/viewed.

■ The dates and times of previous contacts.

■ Any logging or printouts of communications saved by the victim. (See exhibit 15.)

■ Applicable passwords.

■ Potential suspects.

■ Whether an Order of Protection/restraining order was in effect.

■ Witnesses that may have observed the communication.

■ Whether security software was in use that may have captured additional information.

STOP If the information is still on the screen, photograph and write down verbatim the contents of the communication (scroll if necessary). This may be the only opportunity to capture the contents of the communication as this information may be lost when power is disconnected.

Exhibit 15. **Message logging**

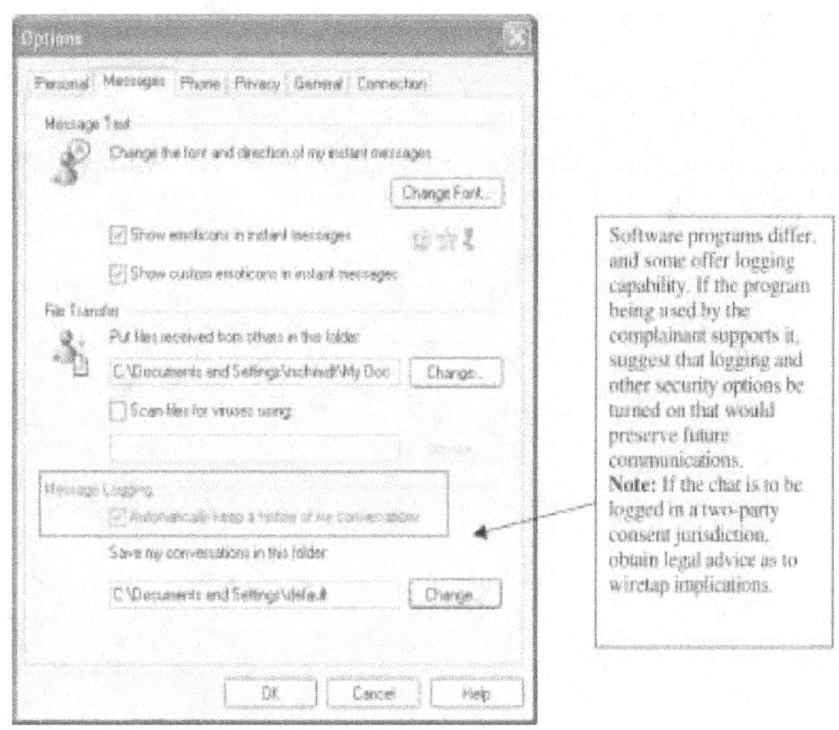

Although some IM services have the ability to log information on the user's hard drive, this logging is frequently not enabled. Realize that a forensic examination of the complainant's computer may provide the only evidence related to the crime. The decision to collect the complainant's computer will depend on the circumstances of the investigation.

The investigator should consider whether—

■ The severity of the complaint warrants the collection of the computer and submission for forensic examination.

■ The complainant may be inconvenienced while the system is in law enforcement's possession.

■ The suspect may notice that the complainant is not online and the investigation may be compromised.

Additional evidence may also be found on other computer systems or devices used by the suspect. See *Electronic Crime Scene Investigation: A Guide for First Responders* (www.ojp.usdoj.gov/nij/pubs-sum/187736.htm) for information on collecting and preserving computer evidence.

Once a suspect's screen name is identified, a computer unrelated to the investigation can be used to identify if an online "profile" is associated with the screen name. The profile might include pictures and other information that would assist in identifying the suspect. (See exhibit 16.)

Service providers are not required to retain IP address information. Therefore, when an IM program is involved, time is of the essence. A preservation letter should be sent to the messenger service provider to maintain information while additional legal steps are pursued. Refer to chapter 9 for further discussion on preservation letters.

Chat rooms

Chat rooms are similar to IM services in that they allow users to communicate in real time. However, instant messaging is usually one to one, whereas chat rooms are usually a group conversation involving two or more people. Certain software programs or ISPs provide lists of chat rooms based on areas of interest or topics of discussion. Users may have unrestricted access to these chat rooms or the chat rooms may be restricted by size (number of participants) or password.

Chat sessions may be monitored and logged by the service provider, providing a potential witness and documented content of the sessions. However, log retention varies depending on the service provider and time is of the essence. A preservation letter should be sent to the chat service provider to maintain information while additional legal steps are pursued. Refer to chapter 9 for further discussion on preservation letters.

In chat rooms, a screen name might not be permanently reserved for a specific individual and therefore cannot be relied on to identify a person. Each user in a chat room must

Exhibit 16. Profile screen

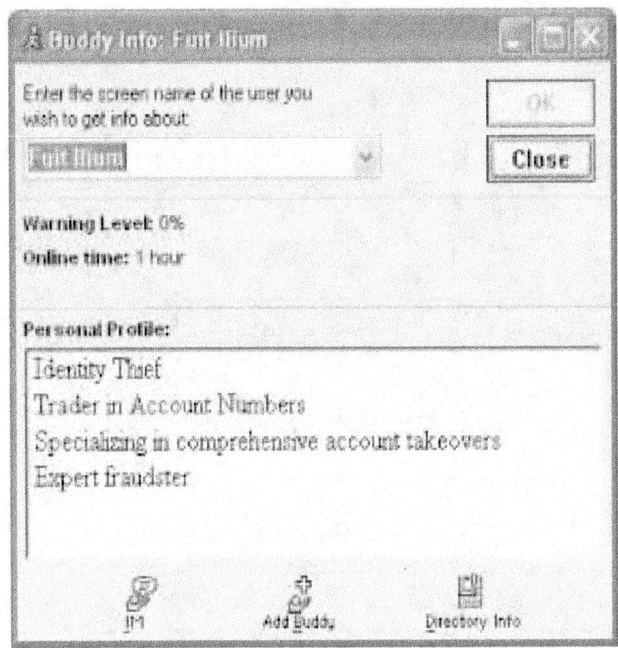

have a unique screen name for that session. However, when that individual logs off, that screen name may be available for use by another individual. In addition, different individuals can use the same screen name at the same time if they are in different chat rooms. Just because the same screen name is seen in a chat room on another occasion does not necessarily mean the same user was using that screen name at the time the original complaint was received. Exhibit 17 shows a chat room screen.

Investigations involving chat rooms

Many of the steps followed when investigating chat rooms are similar to those used when investigating crimes involving IM services. The following may be relevant information to obtain in a chat room investigation:

- Name of the chat room.

- Web address of the chat room.

- Computer being used to receive the communication.

- Screen or user name (victim and suspect).

Exhibit 17. **Chat room screen**

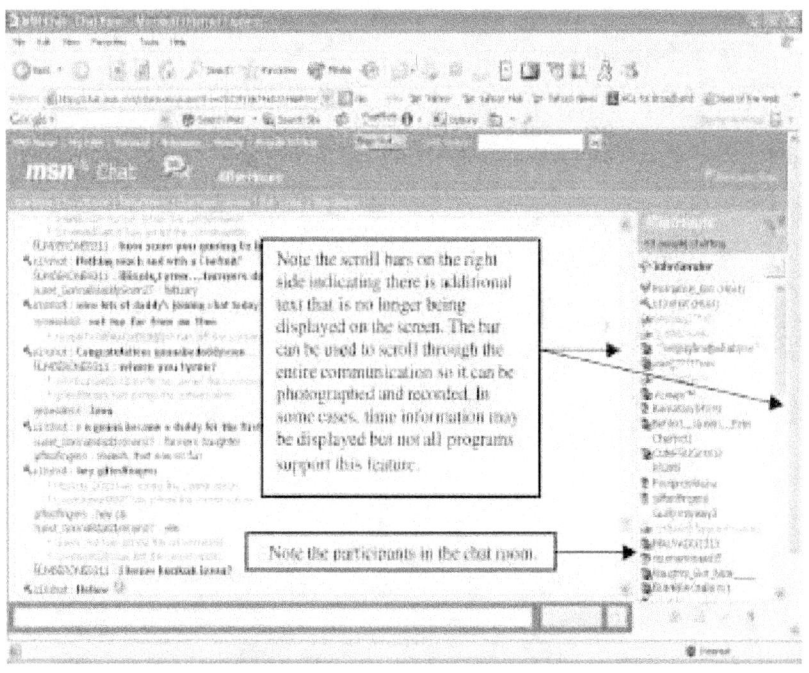

- Owner of the ISP account being used.

- Chat software being used, and version of the software.

- Content (witness account of contact or activity).

- Date and time the communication took place.

- Dates and times of previous sessions where similar activity took place.

- Logging or printouts of communications saved by the victim.

- Applicable passwords.

- Potential suspects.

- Order of Protection/restraining order.

- Witnesses.

- Was security software in use that may have captured additional information?

- Did the victim notify the ISP?

- Did the victim capture the IP address?

- Was the chat session monitored? If so, was it reported to the chat monitor and can the chat monitor be identified?

If the program being used by the complainant supports logging and other security options, suggest that they be turned on to preserve future communications.

As with investigations involving IM services, realize that the complainant's computer may contain the only evidence related to the crime. The decision to collect the complainant's computer will depend on the circumstances of the investigation.

Investigative considerations

The investigator should consider whether—

- The severity of the complaint warrants the collection of the computer and submission for forensic examination.

- The complainant may be inconvenienced while the system is in law enforcement's possession.

- The suspect may notice that the complainant is not online and the investigation may be compromised.

Additional evidence may be found on other computer systems or devices used by the suspect and/or other chat room participants. See *Electronic Crime Scene Investigation: A Guide for First Responders* (www.ojp.usdoj.gov/nij/pubs-sum/187736.htm) for information on collecting and preserving computer evidence.

STOP If the information is still on the screen, photograph and write down verbatim the contents of the communication (scroll if necessary). This may be the only opportunity to capture the contents of the communication as this information may be lost when power is disconnected.

Internet Relay Chat

Internet Relay Chat is a virtual gathering place where individuals exchange information. IRC is based on a client-server model. IRC is made up of networked servers, where thousands of individuals use a *"client"* (software program) that connects them to an IRC server through an ISP. Several servers linked together make up a network. Once users connect to an IRC server, they can exchange text-based messages and files in real time with others who also are connected to the same network. (See exhibit 18.) All IRC users connected to the same channel receive the same message, "Hi Folks!"

Exhibit 18. **Internet Relay Chat**

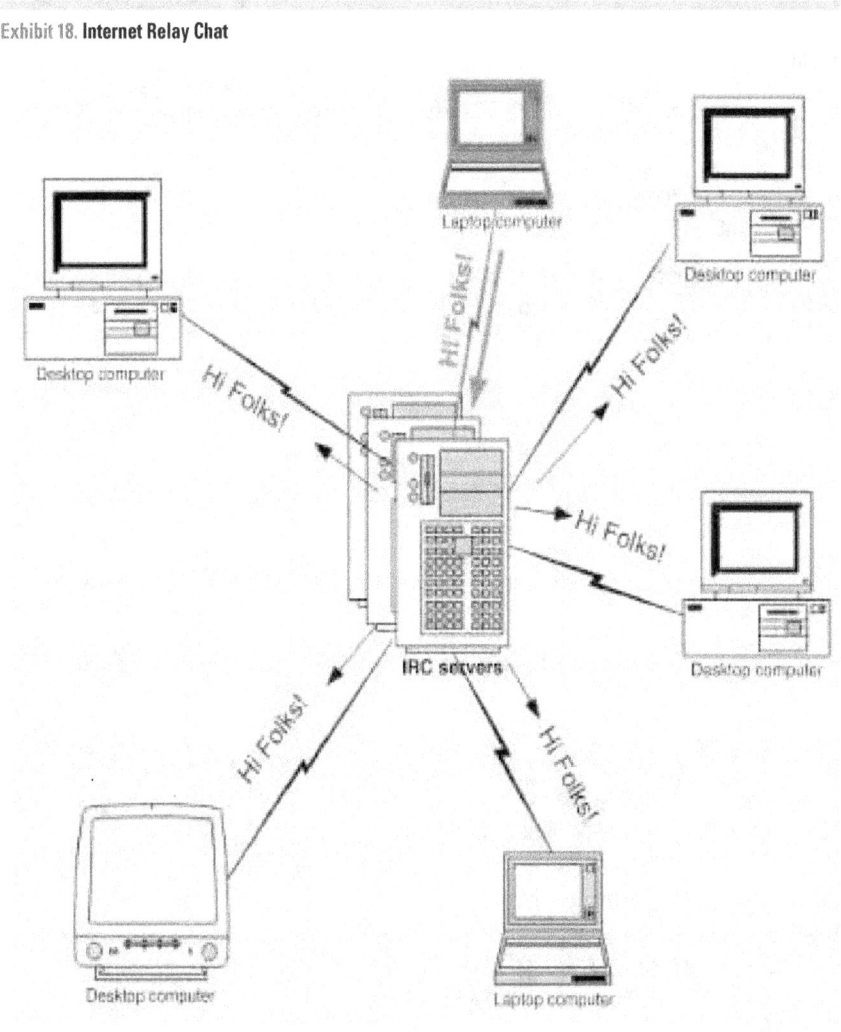

Some of the more popular IRC networks are—

- EFnet   http://www.efnet.org
- Undernet   http://www.undernet.org
- DALnet   http://www.dal.net

The following Web sites can be used as resources to download IRC client software and obtain specific information regarding its use, such as frequently asked questions (FAQs), help guides, user tips, and links to other resources.

- Windows®

  — mIRC   http://www.mirc.com

  — Pirch   http://pirchworld.com

- Linux/Unix

  — Bitch-X   http://bitchx.org

  — Ircii   http://eterna.com.au/ircii/

  — Epic   http://epicsol.org

- Macintosh

  — Ircle   http://www.ircle.com

Client software includes user-configured settings. Examples are—

- ***Port*** number.

- User name.

- E-mail address.

- Nickname(s).

- Internet Protocol address.

- Domain name.

- Logging capabilities.

Nickname

Of significance to the investigator is the user-defined nickname ("nick"). An IRC user must have a nickname, and a common practice is for users to create nicknames that suggest their interests or hobbies. For example: bbsitR ("babysitter"), boylvr ("boy-lover"), or 2yng4u ("too young for you"). Nicknames may be preceded by a special character denoting additional privileges for that user. For example, a channel operator is identified by the "@" symbol in front of his nickname.

A nickname generally is not permanently reserved for a specific individual and therefore cannot be relied on to identify a person. Each user in an IRC network must have a unique nickname while logged on to that network. In most cases, when that individual logs off, that nickname is available for use by another individual. Just because the same nickname is seen in an IRC network on another occasion does not necessarily mean the same user was using the nickname at the time the original complaint was received.

Channels

Channels are "gathering places" for IRC users and are either public (anyone can join) or private (users must use a password key to gain entry or only invitees can join). Users can join more than one channel at a time or create their own channels. Channel names are strings of characters beginning with a "#" or "&."

The first person that joins a channel effectively creates it and is, at least initially, in charge of the channel as a channel operator ("channel-op"). A channel will remain open until the last user exits. Channel operators control the channel settings and can designate other users as channel operators. By default, a channel is public. Any user can type a notice to send to a public channel, acquire a list of its users, or join the conversation. Users can easily be located on IRC unless a user's mode is set to "invisible." Channel operators can change the characteristics of their channel by changing the mode settings. Some settings allow operators to—

■ Make the channel accessible only by invitation.

■ Allow only designated users to be able to post messages.

■ Make a channel private or secret.

■ Ban a user from entering the channel.

Malicious code distribution

IRC servers can also be used by writers of malicious code to gain control over infected computer systems. To accomplish this, the code writer surreptitiously distributes a small program or command to other computers. At specified times, this program causes the infected computer to initiate a connection with an IRC server. Typically, the code writer creates a private IRC channel so that access to the infected computers is limited. Once the connection is created, commands may be given by members of the private channel to the remote computer.

Once control over an infected computer is established, commands can be given that direct the infected computer to send e-mail, transfer files, or probe other computer systems. When a code writer controls hundreds of remote infected computers, commands may be given that cause all of the infected computers to simultaneously send packets to any other computer on the Internet. This is referred to as a Distributed Denial of Service (DDOS) attack. Depending on the number of infected computers and the bandwidth of the victim computer, the DDOS may cause a disruption of service to the victim. See appendix E, sample 4, for a sample case involving an IRC being used by a malicious code writer to control infected computers.

DCC chat

Direct Client to Client (DCC) chat allows two users to communicate directly with each other rather than through the IRC network, making their communication more private. DCC is used for essentially two things: transferring files between two computers and opening a chat link between two computers. (See exhibit 19.)

Exhibit 19. **Direct Client to Client (DCC) chat**

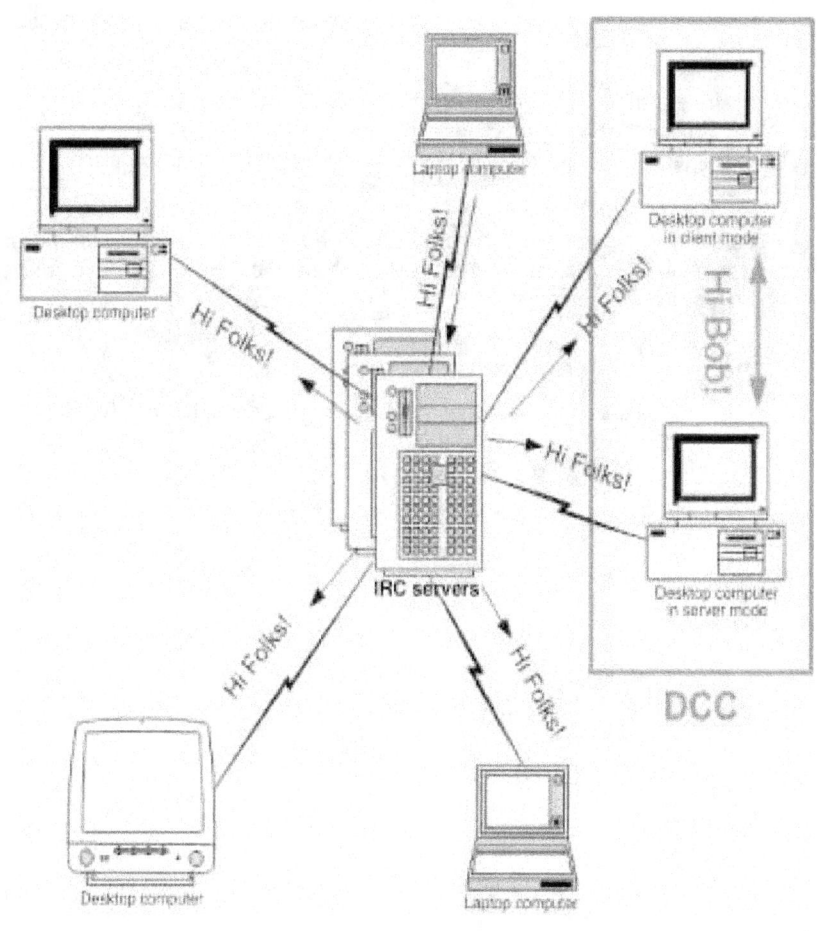

In DCC, the initiating user's host network and IP address are displayed on the screen. If the complainant logged DCC chat sessions, the suspect's IP address may be found in the log files or onscreen if the complainant has not closed out the chat session. (For information on tracing IP addresses, refer to chapter 2.) The sender's host and IP address is underscored in the following example:

> Offering DCC SEND "sexygirl.jpg" connection to Cybercop
> DCC SEND offer from BadBoy (~where@24.41.36.149)
> host:port=192.168.1.100:1024 ("sexygirl.jpg", 1304484 bytes)

File server ("fserv")

IRC users can configure their computers to act as a file server (fserv) to make their collection of images, video clips, audio clips, and other types of files available for others to download via a DCC session.

In channels where an fserv is operational, the fserv owner will post a message. The message provides command line instructions and a description of the files that are available. A user must intentionally initiate a connection to an fserv in order to select a specific file to download.

The IP addresses of the host and client(s) may be found in the log files of the fserv host, the client computer, or onscreen if the chat session has not been closed. (For information on tracing IP addresses, refer to chapter 2.)

Investigative considerations for IRC-related complaints

- What IRC network does the suspect use? (Examples: Undernet, DALnet, EFnet.)

- What nicknames does the suspect use?

- What IRC channels does the suspect use?

- What is the IP address and date and time stamp?

- Was the information on the screen captured and/or documented?

- Did the complainant log or print out any of the following files:

  — Channel chat logs?

  — DCC chat or file transfer logs?

  — E-mail messages?

  — Other documents, images, or files?

- Does the complainant remember the screen names of moderators or any other participants in the channel?

- What IRC server does the suspect use to log on to IRC? (Example: irc.abc.edu.)

- What ISP does the suspect use?

- What time of day is the suspect usually online?

- Does the suspect have channel operator (moderator) status? (May indicate a higher skill level of IRC use.)

- Did the suspect provide any personal identifying information?

Legal issues

Investigations involving IM communications, chat rooms, and IRC may be governed by the Electronic Communications Privacy Act (ECPA), the Fourth Amendment, or appropriate wiretap statutes, depending on the location of the evidence and the timing of its capture. Refer to chapter 9 for discussion of these legal issues.

Summary

IM and chat services allow users to communicate with each other in real time. User profile information provided when subscribers create accounts may be deceptive. The IP address will need to be determined and traced to identify the provider supplying the Internet service. Once the subject user's IP address is identified, subscriber account information may be obtained—with appropriate legal process—from the ISP. Investigators should be aware that a victim's computer might contain the only evidence related to the crime. Care should be taken to record information visible on computer screens and to secure hardware, peripheral media, and software as appropriate. Additional evidence of criminal activity may be found in chat and file transfer logs, e-mail messages, and other data.

Chapter 6. Investigations Involving File Sharing Networks

Investigators increasingly encounter new methods being used to share files containing contraband or illegally obtained data. One fast-growing method being used to commit crimes on the Internet is file sharing networks. The most popular file sharing processes are File Transfer Protocol (FTP) and Peer-to-Peer (P2P) networks. This chapter provides an overview of these technologies. For investigative tips, see appendix D.

File Transfer Protocol

FTP is based on a client-server model that enables a user to transfer files to and from another computer. Any computer can act as either a client or a server. FTP sites can be configured to allow an anonymous connection or require a user name and password. Some common FTP client programs include Web browsers, WS-FTP (Light Edition & Pro), War FTP Daemon, CuteFTP, BulletProof FTP, and FTP Voyager. The client-server model is similar to a central file cabinet in an office where people can access documents. (See exhibit 20.)

Exhibit 20. **FTP**

FTP scenario

Fred searches the chat channels and news groups to find the addresses of FTP servers that are sharing music. He uses an FTP client program to connect to the FTP server address he has found. He reviews the music available and if he finds the song he wants, he downloads the song.

Peer-to-Peer

A true P2P network shares information directly between computers and does not require a server. In the file sharing P2P networks such as Kazaa, Grokster, Morpheus™, or Blubster™, users searching for a desired file query a directory that is stored on a server. (**Note:** The server does not usually maintain audit logs of file transfer activity.) The directory points the user to the computer or multiple computers where the actual file is stored. The user then downloads the file directly from one or more computers on a P2P network that contains the file. The structure of a P2P network changes as computers enter and leave the network, so a P2P network is in a constant state of change. (See exhibit 21.)

Many P2P applications exist; some of the more popular applications include Kazaa, Grokster, Morpheus™, Blubster™, WinMX™, iMesh, Filetopia, eDonkey, and Freenet.

Exhibit 21. P2P Network

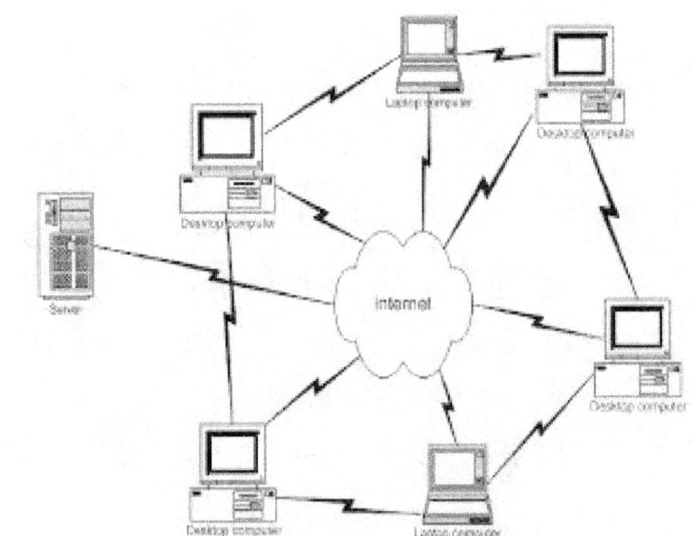

Simple P2P scenario

Fred wants to obtain child pornography. Fred starts up Kazaa file sharing and searches other Kazaa users for the common child pornography term "Lolita." Users on the Kazaa network normally have a directory of items they share to the network. Fred finds numerous files that match his search term and transfers them to his computer directly from the source(s).

Investigative considerations for file sharing networks

FTP and P2P file sharing networks have valid uses, but they also enable users to easily search for, obtain, possess, and/or distribute a variety of illegal content. An individual who uses FTP or P2P may possess a combination of illegal material and illegally obtained data, such as—

■ Child pornography.

■ Copyrighted material (music, movies, video games, photographs, software).

■ Intellectual property/trade secrets.

■ Financial information (credit card numbers, bank account information).

■ Personal identifying information (social security number, date of birth, driver's license).

As users become more sophisticated, they may develop other techniques to mask their true identity. Among these techniques are the use of proxy servers.

Complex P2P scenario—proxy server

Fred, who does not want to be traced back to his work computer, searches the Internet for free proxy services. Fred starts up the Kazaa program, configures it to use a free proxy server Internet Protocol (IP) address, then searches for the term "Lolita." Fred finds files that match "Lolita" and starts transferring the files to his computer via the proxy server. If an investigator tries to find Fred by tracing Fred's IP address, the investigator will only be able to trace the IP address to the proxy server. However, if the proxy server maintains logs, the investigator may be able to obtain information that may identify Fred's true IP address. At times, though, the proxy server may be located in another country, or logs may not be available. (See exhibit 22.)

Investigations of crimes involving file sharing networks can be complex, requiring additional resources and expertise. The first step in these investigations is to determine the IP address of the suspect computer. The address of the suspect computer may be obtained from the complainant's Internet Service Provider (ISP) by forensic examination of the complainant's computer or through the use of proactive undercover techniques. Undercover techniques are beyond the scope of this special report. Some file sharing applications provide anonymity by using **redirectors** and proxy servers and can disguise a user's location from other users and investigators.

Exhibit 22. **Proxy server scenario**

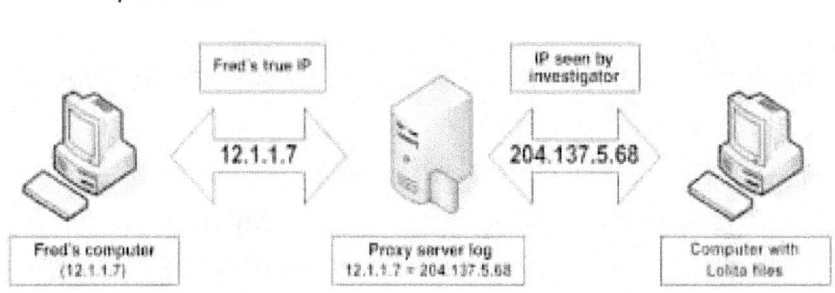

Forensic exam evidence

Evidence the investigator can obtain from a computer forensic exam includes—

- Files that are either contraband or illegally possessed.

- Configuration files showing server or user information, connection history, shared drives on a network, or Internet sites that provide offsite data storage space (e.g., X-Drive, Yahoo!® Briefcase, .Mac, etc.).

- Data files showing file sharing locations with user names, passwords, search terms, file listings, and date and time information (.db, .dbb).

- Log files that show transfers and network activity.

- Stored e-mail that shows relevant user activity.

- File transfer programs.

ISP evidence

Evidence the investigator can obtain from the suspect's ISP:

- Firewall, Dynamic Host Configuration Protocol (DHCP), and *RADIUS logs,* which may assist in connecting the suspect to the illegal activity.

- E-mail server logs, payment records, and subscriber information, which may assist in identifying the suspect and in connecting the suspect to the illegal activity.

Legal issues

Investigations involving file sharing networks may be governed by the Electronic Communications Privacy Act (ECPA), the Fourth Amendment, or appropriate wiretap statutes, depending on the nature of the investigation and location of the evidence. Refer to chapter 9 for discussion of these legal issues.

Summary

This chapter introduces the concept of file sharing networks. FTP and P2P networks allow users to share files. FTP client programs enable users to download files from a central server, whereas P2P client programs allow users to exchange files directly between computers. FTP and P2P network users can obscure their true IP addresses through the use of proxy servers, which means that those server logs must be obtained in a timely manner.

Chapter 7. Investigations of Network Intrusion/Denial of Service

This chapter is intended to be a resource for the investigation of a network intrusion or a Denial of Service (DoS) attack. Since intrusions and DoS attacks are frequently implemented by the use of a ***virus, worm, Trojan,*** or script, a brief discussion of these programs is included. Network investigations can be very complex and may require additional expertise beyond the scope of this special report. Obtaining contact information for such resources prior to conducting an investigation is beneficial. However, some basic steps can be taken to identify what occurred and to preserve the evidence for further investigation.

What is a network?

A network at its most basic level is two or more devices connected in some way using hardware and software to enable the devices to communicate. Devices such as (but not limited to) computers, printers, routers, switches, wireless devices, access points, laptops, and personal digital assistants can be nodes on networks. A node is a network component that performs network-related functions and is treated as a single entity. Connection media between nodes may include wire cable (twisted pair, untwisted pair, coax), fiber optic, wireless, microwave, infrared, or satellite. The way a network is configured in terms of nodes and connections is referred to as its architecture. Network architecture can range from two devices connected to each other in one location to hundreds of thousands of devices connected across many geographically dispersed locations. Any node on a network may be an important source of evidence when investigating a network-based crime.

Viruses, worms, and Trojans

Viruses, worms, and Trojans are generally malicious programs ***(malware)*** that cause an unexpected and frequently undesirable action on a victim's system. A virus is an executable file designed to spread to other computers without detection. It can be transmitted as an attachment to e-mail, as a download, or be present on a diskette or CD. A worm is a type of virus that self-replicates across a network, consuming system resources and slowing or halting the system. A Trojan is a malicious code concealed within an apparently harmless program that hides its true function.

Scripts

A script is a file that automates the execution of a series of commands. Network administrators often use scripts to facilitate completion of a task such as creation of user accounts or the implementation of security updates. Scripts are easily obtained, often shared via the Internet, and can be used by individuals with limited computer knowledge. Scripts can be used to discover and exploit a network's vulnerabilities.

Network intrusion

An intrusion is the unauthorized access or access in excess of a user's privileges on a network. An intrusion is usually accomplished by taking advantage of a system that is not properly configured, a known vulnerability that was not patched, or weak security implementation such as a blank or easily guessed password. Once access to the network has been gained, the intruder(s) can exploit the system in various ways. Some examples include—

- Intelligence gathering.

- Determining user accounts and passwords.

- Network mapping.

- Creating additional accounts or access paths *(backdoors)* for later use.

- Escalating user privileges.

- Using *sniffer* software to monitor network traffic.

- Using network resources to store and/or share files.

- Gaining access to proprietary or confidential data.

- Theft or destruction of data.

- Using resources to identify and exploit other vulnerable systems.

Denial of Service

A Denial of Service attack is an action (or actions) designed to disrupt the target system's ability to provide network services and prevent users from accessing resources. A common DoS attack generates a flood of data, placing an overwhelming demand on a system's resources so that it cannot respond to legitimate requests. Although frequently intentional, a DoS can also occur unintentionally through a misconfigured system.

Investigating intrusions and DoS attacks

One of the first steps taken in any investigation is to identify individuals who have information relating to the incident. In a network investigation those individuals may include—

- Network administrators.

- Employees, current or former.

- Network users.

- Internet Service Providers.

- Consultants.

- Information technology manager(s).

- Human resources.

- Account managers.

STOP Be aware that any of the above listed individuals may be a potential suspect or may not be forthcoming in providing accurate information.

Additional information to gather from the victim includes—

- Economic impact of the incident.

- Network security measures in place at the time of the incident.

Identification of the network architecture also is important. Usually the network administrator will be able to provide information on the devices connected to the network, their physical location, and the way they are connected. Other sources of evidence to consider include—

- Locally connected computers and servers.

- Remote users and devices.

- External network service providers.

  — Offsite storage.

  — Application service providers.

  — Offsite backup service providers.

Note: Keep in mind that devices containing evidence may be in different buildings, States, or countries.

The system administrator should be able to provide information on any system management tools or security measures that were in place at the time of the incident, the types of logs that were being maintained, and backup logs from the time of the incident. Examples of information that can be obtained from logs include whether—

- Accounts were added.

- Files were added, modified, copied, or deleted.

- Security settings were reconfigured or backdoors added.

- Virus or Trojan activity is indicated.

- Intrusion and sniffer tools were copied to the network.

- Internet Protocol addresses of the apparent perpetrators were logged.

- Services were stopped or started.

- Ports were closed or opened.

- Other relevant activity occurred.

STOP If logging has not been turned on, suggest the victim enable logging to collect any potential evidence from future occurrences.

STOP In many network investigations, the reporting entity is the victim. The investigator should be aware of the repercussions of any actions taken in the collection of evidence. Depending on the situation, the investigative response could be as simple as the collection and examination of log files, or as complex as bringing in a network computer forensic expert who may shut down the entire network and image the systems. Be aware that shutting down the network could result in significant loss of revenue.

Wireless networks

While many networks use some type of physical cable connection for communication, wireless networks using radio signals to communicate have become quite popular. A wireless network is a simple and inexpensive method of sharing resources that does not require a hard-wired connection. However, the use of a wireless network requires the user to be in the proximity of the wireless access point. The strength of the wireless signal that is transmitted will determine how close a user must be to use the network resources.

Depending on the configuration, users may be able to connect to a wireless network without the knowledge of the network owner simply by being close enough to the signal. For example, "war driving" refers to driving through a neighborhood with a wireless-enabled device in order to identify wireless access points. Wireless "hot spots" are now available in many public locations such as airports, coffee shops, book-stores, and fast food restaurants.

Information to collect during a wireless network investigation may include whether—

- The Service Set Identifier (SSID) was being broadcast. The SSID is an identifier included in packets to allow the differentiation between multiple wireless networks. All access points and all devices using a specific wireless network must use the same SSID.

- Wired Equivalent Privacy (WEP) was enabled. WEP is a form of encryption that is used to protect wireless communication from eavesdropping and to prevent unauthorized access to a wireless network.

- Dynamic Host Configuration Protocol (DHCP) was enabled and if logs are available. When DHCP is enabled, a system is automatically configured and allowed to connect to the network.

- Logs were maintained of wireless connections that were established.

This information will help determine how vulnerable the network was to an intrusion. If the above security measures were implemented, a nonauthorized user would require special knowledge and/or tools to gain access.

Note: This chapter provides an introduction to network investigations. By nature, this type of investigation is technically complex and is likely to require the assistance of specialized experts in the field. Vulnerabilities and exploits are continually discovered and information on these issues is made available by several organizations including SANS (www.sans.org) and CERT (www.cert.org). Information related to viruses, Trojans, and worms is provided by antivirus software producers, such as Symantec (www.symantec.com), Computer Associates (www.ca.com), and F-Secure (www.fsecure.com).

Legal issues

Network investigations may raise issues concerning the Fourth Amendment, Electronic Communications Privacy Act (ECPA), and the Privacy Protection Act. These issues are discussed in more depth in chapter 9 of this publication; in another publication in this series, *Digital Evidence in the Courtroom: A Guide for Law Enforcement and Prosecutors* (www.ojp.usdoj.gov/nij/pubs-sum/211314.htm); and in the U.S. Department of Justice, Computer Crime and Intellectual Property Section's white paper entitled *Searching and Seizing Computers and Obtaining Electronic Evidence in Criminal Investigations* (July 2002) (www.cybercrime.gov/s&smanual2002.htm).

Summary

This chapter provides details regarding methods used in network intrusions and Denial of Service. The concept of file sharing networks covers File Transfer Protocol (FTP) and Peer-to-Peer (P2P) networks. Viruses, worms, and Trojans are generally malicious programs that can cause an unexpected and frequently undesirable action on a system. A script is a file that automates the execution of a series of commands, and an intrusion is the unauthorized access or access in excess of a user's privileges on a network. Considerations are provided on network investigations and include information on physical cable connection as well as wireless connections for communication. One of the first steps taken in any investigation is to identify individuals who have information relating to the incident.

Chapter 8. Investigations Involving Bulletin Boards, Message Boards, Listservs, and Newsgroups

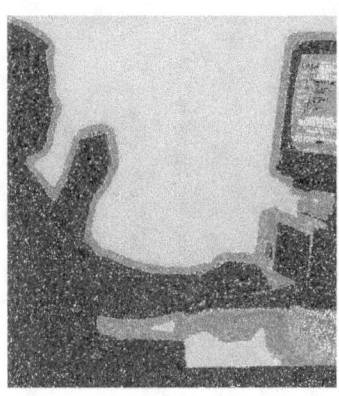

Although electronic mail and instant messaging have become increasingly popular, other forms of electronic communication, some dating to the 1960s, remain in active use among certain users with specialized interests. Because these older electronic communication services may be used to further criminal activities, such as fraud and child exploitation, investigators should know how these systems work and how to gather evidence from them.

When investigating offenses involving the Internet, time, date, and time zone information may prove to be very important. Server and computer clocks may not be accurate or set to the local time zone. The investigator should seek other information to confirm the accuracy of time and date stamps.

Bulletin Board Services

Before the Internet became a mainstream communications medium, computer users often communicated directly with one another via modems and Bulletin Board Services (BBS) programs. These connections are not relayed by way of the Internet. They are private communications established over common telephone lines directly between two computers.

The BBS communications, while generally slower than the Internet, do not require an Internet connection. In order to access a BBS, a computer and modem are used to dial a telephone number to establish a connection with the BBS hosting computer. Typically, the BBS host authenticates (through user name and password) whether the user is authorized to use the system. After entry into the system, access is allowed to uploaded files and posted messages. Groups of associated messages and responses constitute discussion *"threads."*

The BBS host has absolute control over users allowed on the system. For example, the BBS host can set different access levels within the BBS, allowing only the most trusted users access to the most sensitive information. Therefore, in some cases, the investigator may need to gain the confidence of the BBS operator to access certain areas within the BBS. Since the connection between the two computers is not Internet based, Internet-related investigative tools and techniques will not work in the BBS environment.[12]

---

[12]Some Internet-based programs emulate the BBS applications. In these situations, follow normal Internet-based investigative techniques. See chapter 4.

Important information to consider in the initial stages of a BBS investigation includes—

- What is the phone number of the BBS? (If Web site, refer to chapter 4.)

- What is the name of the BBS?

- What was the date and time of the activity?

- Are logs available from the BBS server?

- Where is the BBS located?

- What software is in use by the BBS?

- What is the user ID and password for accessing the BBS?

- What is expected to be found (graphics, text messages, etc.)?

Message boards

Message boards are based on the World Wide Web at services such as Yahoo!® Groups (Groups.Yahoo.com) or Topica.com. Users can log in after obtaining a user ID and password (in most cases) and post information on a given topic. In some cases, users can read but not post messages on Web-based message boards without logging in to the systems that host the boards. Often the messages will not be found by search engines but will only be accessible through direct access to the message board service. For example, messages posted on a Yahoo!® private message board can only be viewed by members of that particular board. Since message boards are Web based, evidence can be preserved in the same manner as a standard Web site investigation (see chapter 4).

To identify the individual who posted a message, the originating Internet Protocol (IP) address may be subpoenaed or obtained with appropriate legal process, which can identify the Internet Service Provider (ISP). A separate legal process may then be needed to obtain user or account information.

Postings to message boards may contain the originating IP address or e-mail address of the individual, commonly known as the "poster." In these cases, issuing a subpoena or appropriate legal process directly to an ISP may identify the posters. Note that the information provided by posters could be fictitious and/or in some cases may be altered by individuals who have access to the posting. The service provider is not likely to retain information regarding users who only visit the board without logging in. Service providers have differing retention periods for logs and other information that may be of interest to investigators.

Questions in message board investigations

When investigating message boards, a number of important pieces of information can be obtained. Among some of the questions to be answered are—

- What is the name of the message board?

- What is the URL of the message board?

- Who hosts the message board?

- Is authorization required for membership?

- Is there a password and/or user ID?

- Can the investigator gain access?

- Is a guest account available?

- What is the user name of the suspect?

- What type of message board management software was used?

- Is the message board moderated? If yes—

  —Who are the moderators?

- Are archives available?

  —Who has copies?

  —Did any participants maintain their own archive?

- Is date and time information correct on the hosting server?

- How did the complainant discover the message board?

- How long and to what extent has the complainant used the message board?

- What is the complainant's user name on the message board?

- Who are the other members on the message board?

- Is other information known about the suspect?

- Has the complainant had other forms of contact with the suspect?

STOP If investigators need to access the message board to answer the above questions, keep in mind that identifying information about the investigator's computer may be revealed and can compromise the investigation.

Listservs

Listservs are popular among special interest groups seeking an efficient and inexpensive way to communicate with large groups of people. A group's listserv is an e-mail-based service that allows a subscriber to send an e-mail to a single address for distribution to all subscribers. Listserv software provides a central point of administration for the distribution of e-mail. Listservs can be publicly accessible or privately administered, allowing a moderator to control access and content. Some listservs are Web based, such as Yahoo!®Groups or Topica, while others exist on private mail servers, using such software as "Mailman" or "L-soft."

A listserv allows subscribers to send bulk electronic mail to all members of the group with both individual messages and digests containing multiple messages. In some cases, subscribers are allowed to upload and download files from designated file storage areas or send and receive files as attachments, which are subsequently stored on the mail server.

Although the network administrator of the hosting server will have ultimate control over the operations of a listserv, the person responsible for the configuration of an individual listserv is the list administrator or list owner. The list owner designates moderators and assigns them administration rights, such as adding and deleting users and approving messages for distribution on a moderated list.

Because listservs have multiple layers of information, the investigation may require a combination of Web, e-mail, and message board investigative techniques.

Questions in listserv investigations

When investigating listservs, a number of important pieces of information can be obtained. Some of the questions to be answered are—

- What is the name of the listserv?

- Who hosts the listserv, and on what mail server?

- What listserv software was used?

- Who is the list administrator (owner)?

- Is the listserv moderated? If yes—

  — Who are the moderators?

- Are archives available?

  — Who has copies?

  — Did any participants maintain their own archive?

- What is the e-mail address of the sender?

- Is a message "header" available? (See chapter 3 for details.)

- How did the complainant first find out about this listserv?

- How long has the complainant used the listserv?

- What is the complainant's e-mail address?

- Who are the other members on the listserv?

- Are other e-mail addresses used by the suspect?

- Has the complainant had other forms of contact with the suspect?

  — E-mail, telephone, instant messaging?

- Is the identity of the suspect known? How?

- Is other contact information or biographical information about the suspect available?

Newsgroups

Newsgroups are large messaging systems that consist of text messages and encoded files (e.g., pictures, sounds, movies, programs) organized into categories of interest with multiple subcategories and topics. The Usenet, which is the Internet network where newsgroups are structured, hosts hundreds of thousands of newsgroups at any given time. The news service provider, usually the user's ISP, determines the newsgroups available on any particular news server. Free news servers also are available but usually provide access to a limited number of news groups. Subscription news servers are available that provide access to an unlimited number of news groups.

Newsgroups currently operate using the Internet and a protocol, or a set of operating specifications, known as Network News Transfer Protocol (NNTP). This protocol is similar to the e-mail protocol (SMTP). Message headers for newsgroup postings can be traced in a manner similar to e-mail headers (see chapter 3). Newsgroup servers are computers that usually are interconnected and store newsgroup messages for distribution to users. Users can participate passively by reading the contents of the group postings, or participate actively by posting or requesting information from other users.

Some newsgroups are moderated and therefore cannot be posted to by individuals— articles posted to them must be mailed to a moderator who will post them for the submitter. The presence of a moderator may provide another investigative lead. In an unmoderated newsgroup, the message is posted directly without editing. The majority of newsgroups are unmoderated.

Usually newsgroups are accessed via a special program called a newsgroup "client" or "reader." Some browsers and e-mail clients also contain newsgroup readers. Examples of newsgroup readers include—

- FortéAgent/Free Agent.

- Outlook®/Outlook Express®.

- Netscape®.

Usenet newsgroups consist of discussions on any conceivable topic. For example, a new scuba diver, looking for other divers with whom to share an experience, subscribes to a newsgroup entitled "rec.scuba." Law enforcement can use newsgroups to locate victims, develop leads, exchange information, and proactively investigate a wide range of potential criminal activities and trends.

Newsgroups also can serve as a communications medium to facilitate a wide range of criminal activities, including—

■ Disseminating child pornography.

■ Distributing pirated software, movies, and music.

■ Obtaining plans for destructive devices.

■ Sharing hate-motivated writings.

■ Organizing gang activities.

■ Distributing information regarding insider stock trading (or posting false information to further stock trading fraud schemes).

Newsgroup scenario of financial fraud

An individual seeking to perpetrate a stock trading scheme logs on to an online investor newsgroup and attempts to remain anonymous using an alias. He participates in discussions on the newsgroup for several weeks and builds a relationship with the other users while simultaneously participating in other groups in which he obtains tips on prior schemes from other offenders. He then provides fake documents and false information, including links to bogus Web sites or false e-mails he created, in an effort to manipulate a stock price.

Questions in newsgroup investigations

When investigating newsgroups, a number of important pieces of information can be obtained. Among some of the questions to be answered are—

■ What is the name of the newsgroup?

■ What is the e-mail address of the poster?

■ Is a message "header" available?

 — What is the NNTP-Posting-Host?

 — What is the date and time of the post?

 — What is the message ID number?

 — Where did the message originate?

■ How did the complainant first find out about this newsgroup?

■ How long has the complainant used the newsgroup?

■ What is the complainant's e-mail address?

■ Are other e-mail addresses used by the suspect?

- Is the identity of the suspect known? How?

- Is other contact information or biographical information about the suspect available?

Newsgroup message headers

A standard Usenet message consists of header lines followed by the body of the message. The header is similar to the e-mail header previously discussed in chapter 3. Exhibit 23 is an example of a newsgroup message header.

Exhibit 23. **Newsgroup message header**

```
Path:news-hub.dragnet.net!news-lhr.fgannon.net!newsjfriday714-
gui.server.ntli.net!news.markiv.net!postmark.nist.gov!pushme.nist.gov!no
t-for-mail
From:Nist@Nist.gov
Newsgroups:alt.rec.scuba
Subject:Testing Post for NIST
Date:Tue,13Aug2002 04:17:00 -0500 (UTC)
Organization:subscriberofnistgov
Lines:32
Message-ID:<ajaiqc$k1n$1445@pushme.nist.gov>
NNTP-Posting-Host:adsl226.dyn996.pushme.nist.gov
X-Trace:pushme.nist.gov. 1029230220 20535 129.6.16.92(13Aug2002 04:17:00
EDT)
X-Complaints-To:abuse@pushme.nist.gov
NNTP-Posting-Date:Tue,13Aug2002 04:17:00 -0500 (UTC)
X-Received-Date:Tue,13Aug2002 04:22:29 EDT (news-hub.dragnet.net)
Xref:news-hub.dragnet.net alt.rec.scuba:363129
```

To understand the parts of the newsgroup message header in exhibit 23, a line-by-line description follows.

**Path:news-hub.dragnet.net!news-lhr.fgannon.net!newsjfriday714-
gui.server.ntli.net!news.markiv.net!postmark.nist.gov!pushme.nist.gov!not-for-mail**
This is the path the message took to reach the current system. When a system forwards the message, it adds its own name to the list of systems in the front of the "Path" line. The system names may be separated by any punctuation character or characters except "." which is considered part of the hostname.

Additional names are added from the left. A host adds its own name to the front of a path when it receives a message from another host. For example, the most recently added name in the above path statement is news-hub.dragnet.net.

Normally, the rightmost name will be the name of the originating system. However, it is also permissible to include an extra entry on the right, which is the name of the sender (e.g., not-for-mail indicates that the sender's name was not translated by the server). Some Usenet software limits the size of the path in the header. Therefore, the originating

server entry may have been lost if the path exceeds this limit and the entry "path truncated" may appear.

From:Nist@Nist.gov
The e-mail address of the original poster. It may also contain a name or nickname created by the poster of the message. This information is generated by the client and may not reflect an accurate name or e-mail address.

Newsgroups:alt.rec.scuba
The name(s) of the newsgroup(s) to which the message was posted.

Subject:Testing Post for NIST
The message topic generated by the poster.

Date:Tue,13Aug2002 04:17:00 -0500 (UTC)
The date and time that the message originated. This information is typically generated by the server. **Note:** *An offset from UTC is sometimes displayed in the following format: 13 Aug 2002 04:17:00 -0500. The "-0500" in the example indicates that the time the message was posted to the server is Eastern Daylight Time – UTC minus 5 hours.*

Organization:subscriberofnistgov
A short phrase describing the organization to which the sender belongs, or to which the machine belongs. The intent of this line is to help identify the organization of the person posting the message, since host names are often cryptic enough to make it hard to recognize the organization by the electronic address. If the entry is blank when the message is received into the NNTP network, a generic entry is made by the receiving server.

Lines:32
This contains a count of the number of lines in the body of the message, excluding header.

Message-ID:<ajaiqc$k1n$1445@pushme.nist.gov>
The "Message-ID" line is a unique identifier followed by the full domain name of the host where the message entered the network.

NNTP-Posting-Host:adsl226.dyn996.pushme.nist.gov
*The IP address or the **fully qualified domain name** of the computer from which the message was received into the NNTP network. It can be the address of the sender, a gateway, or a proxy server used to hide the true sender.*

X-Trace:pushme.nist.gov. 1029230220 20535 129.6.16.92 (13Aug2002 04:17:00 EDT)
The "X-Trace" line is inserted by the server that received the message into the NNTP network. It indicates the fully qualified domain name followed by the date and time that the post was made and the originating IP address. The string of numbers (1029230220) preceding the IP address (129.6.16.92) represents the date as the number of seconds that have passed since January 1, 1970. The remaining number (20535) is the message thread identifier.

X-Complaints-To:abuse@pushme.nist.gov
This line is inserted by the news server and provides an e-mail address for sending complaints on the nature of the message.

NNTP-Posting-Date:Tue,13Aug2002 04:17:00 -0500 (UTC)
Time of the posting to the Usenet.

X-Received-Date:Tue,13Aug2002 04:22:29 EDT (news-hub.dragnet.net)
The date and time the message was received by the server on which that particular newsgroup is hosted.

Xref:news-hub.dragnet.net alt.rec.scuba:363129
This line contains the name of the host and a list of colon-separated pairs of newsgroup names and message numbers. For example, the above "Xref" line shows that the message is message number 363129 in the newsgroup alt.rec.scuba, on host news-hub.dragnet.net.

Note: All header lines may not be displayed by default. Consult the documentation for the particular newsgroup client to determine how to display complete header information.

Investigative steps

Investigative steps are as follows:

■ From the header, identify the newsgroup server to which the message was first posted and the Message-ID.

■ Identify the owner of the domain that hosts the newsgroup server using the "whois" command as described in chapter 2.

■ From the owner of the domain, determine the administrative contact for that newsgroup server.

■ Contact the administrative representative for the newsgroup server. Determine whether server logs were maintained that contain subscriber information or an IP address associated with the Message-ID.

■ Use appropriate legal process to obtain that information.

STOP In many cases logs are not maintained or are only maintained for a short period of time. Therefore, when a newsgroup message is involved, time is of the essence. A preservation letter should be sent to the newsgroup service provider to maintain information while additional legal steps are pursued. Refer to chapter 9 for additional information.

Other techniques to augment the investigation may include searching newsgroup archives, Internet-based e-mail services such as Yahoo!® and Hotmail®, and the World Wide Web for the same or similar user names, e-mail addresses, important keywords, and biographical or other information that may assist in identifying the poster or suspect.

Methods to preserve evidentiary information in newsgroups include—

■ Use software such as SnagIt, Camtasia, PC Pro, and Adobe®Acrobat® to capture screen shots of the messages and headers.

- Photograph newsgroup messages and headers on the screen.

- Use print screen function to capture the contents of messages and their headers and paste each capture individually to another destination file using a program such as WordPad or Paint. **Note:** The print screen function will only capture what is visible. If other portions of the message are required, the screen may need to be scrolled and recaptured.

- Print messages and headers to hardcopy form.

- Search and capture news archives for copies of messages using the methods described above.

Investigative uses of bulletin boards, message boards, listservs, and newsgroups

These technologies can be useful sources of information for an investigator. Their use may—

- Identify additional victims. Victims may post information regarding their victimization and seek out other victims and resources.

- Develop leads. Postings may yield information about how the subject obtained information needed to commit the crime.

- Identify co-conspirators. Threads of prior postings can have biographical or other identifying information for co-conspirators.

- Identify and assist in proving a course of conduct. Threads of discussion can help establish when the criminal venture was created, how it developed, and when it concluded. In addition, evidence of prior acts may exist in prior postings.

- Facilitate proactive investigation. Law enforcement can track postings used in ongoing criminal activity.

Legal considerations

Investigations involving bulletin boards, message boards, listservs, and newsgroups may be governed by the Electronic Communications Privacy Act (ECPA), the Fourth Amendment, or appropriate wiretap statutes, depending on the location of the evidence and the timing of its capture. Refer to chapter 9 for discussion of these legal issues.

Summary

Although newer Internet communication tools are more popular today, earlier forms of digital communication services, including bulletin boards, message boards, listservs, and newsgroups are still in use and may be the subject of criminal investigations.

Bulletin Board Service users establish communication via telephone modem dial-up accounts to remotely access the host server to read or post messages. Standard Internet trace tools may not be of use in obtaining subscriber information. The investigator may be required to covertly access the BBS or obtain telephone records and call data.

Listservs allow multiple subscribers to send bulk e-mail to all members of a group and, in some cases, listservs can allow subscribers to exchange files via a common download site. A combination of Web, e-mail, and bulletin board investigative techniques may be needed to obtain subscriber information.

As is the case with many Internet-based services, subscriber information and digital evidence are volatile. Investigators should move quickly to obtain and preserve evidence.

Chapter 9. Legal Issues

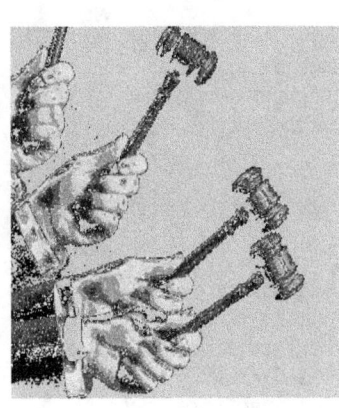

To ensure the admissibility of evidence for a successful prosecution and to avoid civil liability, consideration should be given to the methods and procedures of how evidence is obtained during the investigative process. Constitutional standards, statutory provisions, policies and procedures concerning investigations, and industry-specific acts govern the investigative process. As case law is developed and additional laws and regulations are enacted, other legal requirements may apply. For a more complete discussion of these requirements, refer to another guide in this series, *Digital Evidence in the Courtroom: A Guide for Law Enforcement and Prosecutors* (www.ojp.usdoj.gov/nij/pubs-sum/211314.htm).

Note: A comprehensive analysis of Federal search and seizure issues, *Searching and Seizing Computers and Obtaining Electronic Evidence in Criminal Investigations*, can be found at www.cybercrime.gov/s&smanual2002.htm.

During Internet and network investigations it may be beneficial for the investigator to communicate with Internet and network service providers before serving legal process. The providers may be able to instruct the investigators on available data that would allow the investigator to include the proper wording in the legal documents and any special circumstances or requirements that exist. For example, certain Internet Service Providers (ISPs) have procedures in place to facilitate the issuance of and service of search warrants.

Note: The investigator should be aware that service of legal process on a private company may cause the company to notify the subject that it has received legal process to disclose information about the account.

Preservation letters or orders

Timeliness is critical. Due to the dynamic and temporary nature of digital records, and because of the variability in the duration of time that records are retained by service providers, investigators are encouraged to consider issuing a preservation letter under the provisions of 18 U.S.C. § 2703(f). Generally, no regulations pertain to the retention of records held by service providers. These records may be retained briefly or not at all. The use of a preservation letter or order may be advisable to prevent these records from being destroyed. Although this is a Federal statute, State and local agencies can use this document to preserve digital evidence. Although preservation requests have no legally prescribed format, usually a phone request followed by a faxed letter is sufficient. A sample letter is provided in appendix G.

18 U.S.C. § 2703(f)(1) states: "A provider of wire or electronic communication service or a remote computing service, upon the request of a governmental entity, shall take all necessary steps to preserve records and other evidence in its possession pending the issuance of a court order or other process."

Preservation letters require providers to preserve records that exist at the time the letter is received, but cannot require preservation of future information. On receipt of the preservation letter, the provider must retain records for 90 days. Additional requests may extend the period in increments of 90 days.

Subpoenas

Subpoena requirements vary widely within and between jurisdictions. Additionally, different private organizations may have specific requirements. When drafting a subpoena, specifically define the evidence sought without excluding significant information. It may be advisable to coordinate with your local prosecutor or legal advisor for specific subpoena requirements.

Search warrants

As with subpoenas, requirements for search warrants vary within and between jurisdictions. In all cases, however, probable cause that a crime was committed and that evidence or contraband of that crime exists in the specific location you wish to search should be articulated. The particular evidence or contraband to be seized should be described as well. For further information on drafting a search warrant, refer to *Searching and Seizing Computers and Obtaining Electronic Evidence in Criminal Investigations,* which can be found at www.cybercrime.gov/s&smanual2002.htm. See the Fourth Amendment section in this chapter for further discussion.

STOP During the execution of a search warrant, if evidence is discovered that is not described in the warrant, consider obtaining an additional or amended warrant.

STOP Be cautious when using a template or boilerplate warrant as a guide. Ensure that the warrant fits the specifics of the investigation.

Multijurisdiction issues

Internet and network investigations frequently involve communications that cross local, State, and even international boundaries. As sources of evidence are identified, determine whether the source is located within your State, the United States, or outside the United States.

If you have any suspicion that a source may be located overseas—and this is frequently difficult to discern—stop the search and consult the Computer Crimes and Intellectual Property Section (CCIPS) of the U.S. Department of Justice. CCIPS can be reached 24 hours a day at 202–514–1026.

If the evidence is located outside the United States, immediately contact the relevant country to seek assistance. Such contacts may be made by the investigating agency or through the International Network of 24-hour Points of Contact. CCIPS is the Point of Contact for the United States. The U.S. Department of Justice, Criminal Division, Office of International Affairs (OIA) should also be advised promptly at 202–514–0000.

Foreign assistance with digital evidence may include anything from preserving evidence to immediate disclosure, depending on the facts of the case and which country is involved. OIA and CCIPS can advise on the best approach.

Sometimes evidence may have to be obtained via a Mutual Legal Assistance Treaty or Agreement (MLAT or MLAA).[13] Such requests must go through OIA. If the United States and the relevant country do not have an agreement, procuring the evidence may require the more cumbersome letters rogatory.[14] Both of these processes are time consuming, and often the requested information will take months to receive. However, it may be possible to procure evidence informally for investigative purposes while formal process is pursued to procure evidence in a form usable in court.

Federal law affecting State and local investigators

Investigators, examiners, and prosecutors are encouraged to be familiar with the following Federal requirements, as well as applicable State and local laws, policies, and procedures, because their breach may result in a suppression challenge or civil suit:

- Fourth Amendment.

- Wiretap Act.

- Pen Register and Trap and Trace Statute.

- Electronic Communications Privacy Act (also known as Stored Wire and Electronic Communications Section).

- Privacy Protection Act.

Note: A comprehensive analysis of Federal search and seizure issues, *Searching and Seizing Computers and Obtaining Electronic Evidence in Criminal Investigations*, can be found at www.cybercrime.gov/s&smanual2002.htm.

Fourth Amendment

Searches for digital evidence, like searches for other forms of evidence, are subject to Federal and State constitutional search and seizure laws and court rules. Traditional Fourth Amendment principles, like those governing closed containers, apply to digital evidence.

---

[13] A list of countries that are MLAT and MLAA participants may be found at http://travel.state.gov/mlat.html. A discussion of the MLAT process may be found in the U.S. Attorneys' *Criminal Resource Manual.*

[14] The letters rogatory process is codified at 28 U.S.C. § 1871 *et seq.*

The Fourth Amendment protects individuals from unreasonable searches and seizures. The two primary requirements for Fourth Amendment protections to be invoked are—

■ Is government action involved?

■ Does the person affected have a reasonable expectation of privacy in the place or thing to be searched?

If protections under the Fourth Amendment apply, then law enforcement must obtain a warrant unless an exception exists. Exceptions to securing a warrant include—

■ Consent.

■ Exigent circumstances.

■ Search incident to arrest.

■ Inventory search.

■ Plain view doctrine.

STOP Although the exceptions may provide a legal basis to seize the media containing the digital evidence (e.g., computer, CD-ROM, other storage devices), further legal process may be necessary to conduct a forensic examination of the seized media.

Searches and seizures pursuant to warrants

If the Fourth Amendment applies and none of the warrant exceptions exist, law enforcement agents should obtain a warrant. Generally, the same warrant rules apply when preparing and executing a warrant for digital evidence as for other investigations. Investigators should consider the need to justify searching the contents of the hardware as well as seizing it. Consult legal authority for best practices within a particular jurisdiction.

In preparing the affidavit for a search warrant, consider—

■ What criminal offense is being investigated (e.g., e-mail threats, murder, protection order violation).

■ Specifically where the search will take place (e.g., describe the house, address).

■ What is expected to be found (e.g., hardware, storage devices, manuals, password).

■ How you know it is there (e.g., trace Internet Protocol (IP) address, account names, billing information).

■ Why is it relevant to the crime (e.g., instrumentality, repository, or target of the crime).

Additional considerations in the execution of a search warrant may include—

■ Discovery of evidence outside the scope of the warrant.

— An additional warrant may be necessary or advisable to expand the scope of the original warrant.

■ Reasonable accommodation.

— Minimization of disruption of business.

— Consider the return of noncontraband seized data if commingled with evidence of a crime to accommodate a reasonable request.

Wiretap Act

Omnibus Crime Control and Safe Streets Act of 1968, 18 U.S.C. § 2510 *et seq.*

The Wiretap Act as it applies to Internet and network investigations focuses on the interception of the content of communications while the communications are in transit and governs the disclosure of intercepted communications. Examples of such interceptions may include—

■ Wiretapping a telephone.

■ Real-time network monitoring.

■ Sniffer software.

To ensure compliance, determine whether—

■ The communication to be monitored is one of the protected communications defined in the statute.

■ The proposed surveillance constitutes an "interception" of the communication.

If both conditions are present, consult your local prosecutor or legal advisor for guidance.

Note: Some States have versions of the Wiretap Act that are more restrictive than the Federal act. The Federal act does *not* preempt these laws unless Federal agents are conducting the investigation. State and local law enforcement agents must comply with any such State act, even if there is no violation of the Federal Wiretap Act.

Pen Register and Trap and Trace Statute, 18 U.S.C. § 3121 *et seq.*

The Pen/Trap statute governs the real-time acquisition of dialing, routing, addressing, and signaling information relating to communications. The statute does not cover the acquisition of the content of communications; rather, it covers the transactional information about communications.

A pen register order authorizes the recording of outgoing connection information including every phone number that a specific phone dialed. A pen register order does not authorize the collection of numbers dialed after the connection is established (e.g., account number or PIN) because they constitute content. Conversely, a trap and trace order authorizes the recording of incoming connection information.

The Pen/Trap statute also applies to real-time capture of transactional information related to Internet and network communications. For example, every e-mail communication contains "to" and "from" information. Also, Internet/network packets may contain source and destination addresses.

Note: Some States have versions of the Pen/Trap statute that are more restrictive than the Federal Act. The Federal Act does not preempt these laws unless Federal agents conduct the investigation. State and local law enforcement agents must comply with any such State act, even if there is no violation of the Federal Pen/Trap statute. Consult the local prosecutor or legal advisor for further guidance.

Electronic Communications Privacy Act

Stored Wire and Electronic Communications Section (18 U.S.C. § 2701 *et seq.*)

The stored communications chapter of the Electronic Communications Privacy Act (ECPA) provides customers and subscribers of certain communications service providers with privacy protections. ECPA provides a higher level of privacy protection to the contents of communications and files stored with a provider than to records detailing the use of the service or the subscriber's identity.

ECPA may dictate what type of legal process is necessary to compel a provider to disclose specific types of customer/subscriber information to law enforcement agents. ECPA also limits what a provider may and may not voluntarily disclose to others, including the government.

ECPA applies when a law enforcement agent seeks certain information from a provider of electronic communications service[15] or remote computing service,[16] including—

■ Subscriber information.

■ Transactional information.

■ Content.

ECPA *does not* apply when the agent seeks to obtain information from the customer/subscriber's computer.

---

[15] Section 2510(15), title 18 United States Code, defines electronic communications service as "any service which provides to users thereof the ability to send or receive wire or electronic communications."

[16] Section 2711(2), title 18 United States Code, defines remote computing service as "provision to the public of computer storage or processing services by means of an electronic communications system."

INVESTIGATIONS INVOLVING THE INTERNET AND COMPUTER NETWORKS

Subscriber information

Law enforcement agents may use a subpoena, if allowed by their State law, to obtain certain information listed in ECPA relating to the identity of a customer/subscriber, the customer/subscriber's relationship with the service provider, and basic session connection records. Specifically, a subpoena is effective to compel a service provider to disclose the following information about the customer/subscriber:

- Name.

- Address.

- Local and long distance telephone connection records or records of session times and durations.

- Length of service (including start date) and types of service utilized.

- Telephone or instrument number or other subscriber number or identity, the Internet Protocol address used to establish the account, and any temporarily assigned network IP address.

- The means and source of payment for such service (including any credit card or bank account numbers).

Extensive transaction-related records, such as logging information revealing the e-mail addresses of persons with whom a customer corresponded during prior sessions, are not available by subpoena. However, the use of a subpoena with notice can allow the discovery of the same evidence as a 2703(d) order and should be utilized when seeking this type of information.

Note: Because providers may use different terms to describe the types of data that they hold, it is advisable to consult with each provider about preferred language when drafting the request to maximize the efficiency of obtaining the requested information.

Transactional information

A law enforcement agent will need to obtain a court order under 18 U.S.C. § 2703(d) to compel a provider to disclose more detailed, noncontent subscriber and session information, commonly referred to as transactional information, about the use of the services by a customer/subscriber. These records could include—

- Account activity logs that reflect what IP addresses the subscriber visited over time.

- E-mail addresses of others from whom or to whom the subscriber exchanged e-mail.

Any Federal magistrate or district court with jurisdiction over the offense under investigation may issue a 2703(d) order. State court judges authorized by the law of the State to enter orders authorizing the use of a pen/trap device may also issue 2703(d) orders. The application must offer "specific and articulable facts showing that there are reasonable grounds to believe that . . . the records or other information sought are relevant and material to an ongoing criminal investigation."

A law enforcement agent also can use a 2703(d) order to compel a cellular telephone service provider to turn over, in real time, records showing the cell-site location information for calls made from a subscriber's cellular phone. This information shows more of the subscriber's use of the system than that available by subpoena, but it does not include the content of the communications.

Note: A 2703(d) order also can be used to obtain both subscriber information and transactional information. Refer to *Searching and Seizing Computers and Obtaining Electronic Evidence in Criminal Investigations* (www.cybercrime.gov/s&smanual2002.htm) for examples of applications for an order under 2703(d).

Content

ECPA distinguishes between communications in storage that have already been retrieved by the customer or subscriber and those that have not. The statute also distinguishes between retrieved communications that are held by an electronic communications service, which can be public or private, and those held by a remote computing service, which only provides service to the public.

Retrieved communications, unretrieved communications older than 180 days, and other files stored with a public provider—subpoena with notice or 2703(d) court order with notice, or search warrant. ECPA applies to stored communications that a customer or subscriber has retrieved but left on the server of the communications service provider, if the service provider offers those services to the public. Under the statute, such a provider is considered a "remote computing service" and is not permitted to voluntarily disclose such content to the government unless certain circumstances exist (see 18 U.S.C. § 2702(b) and 18 U.S.C. § 2701(c) for information on the "circumstances"). These communications include any files that a customer may have stored on the public provider's system. If the provider does not offer those services to the public, no constraints are imposed by ECPA on the right of the provider to disclose such information voluntarily.

Note: ECPA may apply if the e-mail sought resides on the employer's server and has not yet been retrieved by the employee. In this instance, the rules discussed under unretrieved communications and search warrants later in this chapter apply.

Prior notice to subscriber. Law enforcement may use either a subpoena or a 2703(d) court order to compel a public service provider to disclose the contents of stored communications that have been retrieved or communications that are unretrieved but have been on the server more than 180 days by a customer or subscriber. In both cases, law enforcement is required to either give prior notice to the subscriber or comply with delayed notice provisions of section 2705(a). Remember, law enforcement can also use a search warrant, which does not require notice to the subscriber to obtain this information.

Note: Section 2705(a) in ECPA allows agents to delay notice to the customer or subscriber when notice would jeopardize a pending investigation or endanger the life or physical safety of an individual. However, pursuant to 2705(b), a "no-notice provision" included with the subpoena or search warrant may prevent the ISP from making disclosure to the subscriber.

Note: If the investigating agency is located within the jurisdiction of the U.S. Court of Appeals for the Ninth Circuit (California, Oregon, Washington, Arizona, Montana, Idaho, Nevada, Alaska, Hawaii, Guam, and the Northern Mariana Islands), the investigator must use a search warrant to compel disclosure of all communications, retrieved or unretrieved. If the investigating agency is located outside the Ninth Circuit, the investigator may follow the traditional ECPA interpretation, under which retrieved communications are available pursuant to a subpoena or 2703(d) court order with notice, even if the provider is located in the Ninth Circuit. However, investigators should be aware that many large providers, including AOL®, Yahoo!®, and Hotmail®, may only provide content information pursuant to a search warrant based on a recent court decision, *Theofel* v. *Farey-Jones,* 359 F.3d 1066 (9th Cir. 2004).

Unretrieved communications. Unretrieved communications (including voice mail) held by the provider for 180 days or fewer have the highest level of protection available under ECPA. ECPA covers such communications whether the service provider is private or public.

Law enforcement may seek a search warrant to compel the production of unretrieved communications in storage with a service provider. No prior notice to the customer/subscriber is required if information is obtained with a search warrant. A search warrant may also be used to obtain subscriber and transactional information.

Voluntary disclosure of electronic communications–18 U.S.C. § 2702(b)(6)(C). Providers of services not available to the public may freely disclose both contents and other records relating to stored communications. ECPA imposes restrictions on voluntary disclosures by providers of services to the public, but it also includes exceptions to those restrictions.

ECPA provides for the voluntary disclosure of contents of electronic communications when the provider "reasonably believes that an emergency involving immediate danger of death or serious physical injury to any person requires disclosure of the information without delay."

See exhibit 24 for ECPA disclosure rules.

Note: Some States may have applicable laws that are more restrictive than ECPA. ECPA does *not* preempt these laws unless Federal agents are conducting the investigation. State and local law enforcement agents must comply with any such State act, even if there is no violation of the Federal statute.

Remedy: civil damages

Civil damages are the *exclusive* remedy for violations of ECPA. ECPA does not contain a provision to suppress evidence obtained in violation of the Act.

Exhibit 24. **Disclosure rules of ECPA**

Type of Information	Voluntary disclosure allowed?		Mechanisms to compel disclosure	
	Public provider	Nonpublic provider	Public provider	Nonpublic provider
Basic subscriber, session, and billing information*	Not to government, unless § 2702(c) exception applies [§ 2702(a)(3)]	Yes [§ 2702(a)(3)]	Subpoena; 2703(d) order; or search warrant [§ 2703(c)(2)]	Subpoena; 2703(d) order; or search warrant § 2703(c)(2)]
Other transactional and account records	Not to government, unless § 2702(c) exception applies [§ 2702(a)(3)]	Yes [§ 2702(a)(3)]	2703(d) order or search warrant [§ 2703(c)(1)]	2703(d) order or search warrant [§ 2703(c)(1)]
Retrieved communications (opened e-mail and voice mail) left with provider and other stored files**	No, unless § 2702(b) exception applies [§ 2702(a)(2)]	Yes [§ 2702(a)(2)]	Subpoena with notice; 2703(d) order with notice; or search warrant [§ 2703(b)]	Subpoena; ECPA doesn't apply [§ 2711(2)]
Unretrieved communication, including e-mail and voice mail (in electronic storage *more than* 180 days)**	No, unless § 2702(b) exception applies [§ 2702(a)(1)]	Yes [§ 2702(a)(1)]	Subpoena with notice; 2703(d) order with notice; or search warrant [§ 2703(a,b)]	Subpoena with notice; 2703(d) order with notice; or search warrant [§ 2703(a,b)]
Unretrieved communication, including e-mail and voice mail (in electronic storage 180 days or fewer)	No, unless § 2702(b) exception applies [§ 2702(a)(1)]	Yes [§ 2702(a)(1)]	Search warrant [§ 2703(a)]	Search warrant [§ 2703(a)]

*See 18 U.S.C. § 2703(c)(2) for listing of information covered. For telephone communications, the section includes, among other records, local and long distance connection records. For Internet connections, the section includes, among others, records of session times and durations and IP addresses assigned to the user during the session.

**For investigating agencies located within the Ninth Circuit, the content of communications may only be obtained with a search warrant under the Ninth Circuit's interpretation of ECPA.

Note: The information in exhibit 24 is taken from page 147 of *Searching and Seizing Computers and Obtaining Electronic Evidence in Criminal Investigations*, www.cybercrime.gov/s&smanual2002.htm.

Privacy Protection Act, 42 U.S.C. § 2000aa *et seq.*

The Privacy Protection Act (PPA) limits law enforcement's use of a search warrant to search for or seize certain materials possessed by a person for the purpose of public dissemination. The intent of this law is to protect publishers from having First Amendment materials seized unless the individual is suspected of harboring illicit material. Generally, this act prohibits the seizure of publication materials by the use of a search warrant with some exceptions. Normally, the government must issue a subpoena. These protected materials may be either "work product" (i.e., materials created by the author/publisher) or "documentary materials" (i.e., any materials that document or support the work product). The term publisher is not limited to the traditional press and may include individuals who have an intent to publish material or have their own Web site.

In assessing the impact of PPA on an investigation, the following factors should be considered:

■ Is the material covered by PPA? PPA-covered material is of two general types:

— Work-product material created for the purpose of disseminating to the public through a public form of communication, 42 U.S.C. § 2000aa-7(b).

— Documentary materials possessed for the purpose of disseminating to the public through a public form of communication, 42 U.S.C. § 2000aa-7(a).

■ Is the possessor of the material covered by PPA? PPA only applies to protect publishers that are innocent third parties. See *S. Rep. No. 96-874* at p. 4 (1980). If the suspect has commingled the publications material with the contraband, a law enforcement agent who seizes the publications material incident to the seizure of the contraband will not be liable under PPA. *Guest* v. *Leis,* 255 F.3d 325 (6th Cir. 2001). However, a law enforcement agent who searches the actual publications material may be liable unless the search is incidental to the search for the contraband material.

PPA's prohibition on the use of a search warrant *does not apply* in the following circumstances:

■ Materials searched for or seized are contraband, fruits, or instrumentalities of the crime.

■ There is reason to believe that the immediate seizure of such materials is necessary to prevent death or serious bodily injury.

■ Probable cause exists to believe that the person possessing the materials has committed or is committing a criminal offense to which the materials relate. (This exception does not apply where the mere possession of the materials constitutes the offense except for the possession of child pornography and certain government information.)

Civil damages are the *exclusive* remedy for violation of PPA. PPA does not contain a provision to suppress evidence obtained in violation of the act.[17]

---

[17] Similar to 42 U.S.C. § 1983, an officer sued in a personal capacity is entitled to a reasonable good faith defense. 42 U.S.C. § 2000aa-6. In addition, the officer may only be sued in his or her individual capacity if the government has not waived sovereign immunity.

Note: For further information on PPA, consult *Searching and Seizing Computers and Obtaining Electronic Evidence in Criminal Investigations* (www.cybercrime.gov/ s&smanual2002.htm).

Other considerations

Privileged or proprietary information

In some instances, law enforcement may have reason to believe that the place to be searched will have information that is considered "privileged" under statute or common law (e.g., when searching the office of a lawyer, doctor, or member of the clergy).[18] Before conducting the search, law enforcement should take care to identify the legal limitations that the jurisdiction may impose and comply with those limitations. Consider in advance whether the evidence to be seized contains privileged or proprietary information.

Juvenile suspects

Investigations involving juvenile suspects are not unusual. If the suspect is a juvenile, this could affect a host of issues, including seizing the computer used in the crime if located in the parent's home, interviewing the juvenile suspect, and charging the juvenile. If the suspect identified is a juvenile, the investigator should be mindful of the effect that a suspect's juvenile status may have on the investigation.

Entrapment and public authority

Internet and network investigations may, under appropriate circumstances, be conducted in a proactive stance. For example, the investigator may assume an undercover status to attempt to have the suspect distribute a contraband file to gather evidence of the suspect's knowledge and intent to control the contraband files. An investigator should be cognizant of his or her jurisdiction's laws regarding entrapment when conducting the investigation in a proactive manner.

Trojan programs

Because investigations involving the Internet and computer networks mean that the suspect's computer communicated with other computers, investigators should be aware that the suspect may assert that the incriminating evidence was placed on the media by a Trojan program. A Trojan is a computer program that may be transferred to an unknowing individual's computer allowing another individual to access the computer system. A proper seizure and forensic examination of a suspect's hard drive may determine whether evidence exists of the presence and use of Trojan programs.

---

[18] Consider obtaining a stipulation before seizing information from the target to avoid confiscating potentially privileged or proprietary information. (See appendix titled "Stipulation Regarding Evidence Returned to the Defendant," from *Digital Evidence in the Courtroom: A Guide for Law Enforcement and Prosecutors.)*

Investigation of trade secret, copyrighted materials, and software piracy file-sharing cases

Some types of file-sharing investigations involve cases where the files themselves are legal, but the suspect's possession or distribution of those files is illegal. In this case the investigating focus will be whether—

- The suspect knew or should have known that the possession and/or distribution of the files was unauthorized.

- The acquisition and distribution chain of the files can be traced.

Federal copyright laws[19] preempt State copyright laws; however, this does not mean that all possible State criminal charges are preempted. Therefore, it is important to consider other applicable State statutes for prosecution such as consumer protection, deceptive trade practice, traditional theft, or larceny statutes.

Summary

Constitutional standards, statutory provisions, policies and procedures concerning investigations, and industry-specific acts govern the investigative process. This chapter briefly addresses some of these aspects. For a more complete discussion of legal aspects relating to digital evidence, refer to another guide in this series, *Digital Evidence in the Courtroom: A Guide for Law Enforcement and Prosecutors* (www.ojp.usdoj.gov/nij/pubs-sum/211314.htm).

---

[19] Federal laws governing copyright of digital intellectual property such as music and movies and criminalizing copyright infringement include the Digital Millennium Copyright Act and the No Electronic Theft Act.

Appendix A. Glossary

ANI: See Automatic Number Identification.

Automatic Number Identification: A service that provides the telephone number of an incoming call.

Backdoor: A backdoor generally circumvents security programs and provides access to a program, an online service, or an entire computer system. It can be authorized or unauthorized, documented or undocumented.

Client: A computer or program that connects to or requests the services of another computer or program. Client also can refer to the software that enables the computer or program to establish the connection.

Clipboard: Temporary computer memory that allows the user to store text and graphics for future use.

DHCP: See Dynamic Host Configuration Protocol

Dynamic Host Configuration Protocol: A service that automates the assignment of Internet Protocol (IP) addresses on a network. DHCP assigns an IP address each time a computer is connected to the network. DHCP uses the concept of a "lease" or amount of time that a given IP address will be valid for a specific computer. DHCP can dynamically reassign IP addresses for networks that have a requirement for more IP addresses than are available.

Firewall: A software program or hardware device that protects the resources of a network from unauthorized access. A firewall filters network packets to determine whether to forward the packets to their requested destination to allow access.

Fully qualified domain name: The hierarchical name of an individual host including the host name along with the full network path to that host (e.g., adsl226.dyn996.pushme.nist.gov).

Gateway: A device that passes traffic between networks. Typically, a gateway physically sits at the perimeter of an internal network to the Internet.

Header: Identifying information transmitted as part of the data packet or as e-mail or newsgroup routing information.

Malware: Computer viruses and other software designed to damage or disrupt a system.

NAT: See Network Address Translation.

Network Address Translation: A service that allows computers on a private network to access the Internet without requiring their own publicly routable Internet Protocol address. NAT modifies outgoing network packets so that the return address is a valid Internet host, thereby protecting the private addresses from public view.

Packet: A transmission unit containing both data and a header that is routed between an origin and a destination on a network.

Point of Presence (POP): A Point of Presence is a physical location that houses servers, routers, ATM switches, and other devices. Not to be confused with Post Office Protocol.

Port: A software-created access point—a "logical connection place"—for moving information into and out of a computer. Each communications service on a computer (e.g., FTP, e-mail, Web) is assigned a port number. Ports are numbered from 0 to 65535. Ports 0 to 1023 are reserved for use by certain privileged services.

Post Office Protocol (POP): A protocol used to retrieve e-mail from a mail server.

Protocol: A standard set of rules that govern how computers communicate or perform a task.

Proxy server: A server that acts as an intermediary between a workstation user and the Internet to facilitate security, administrative control, and caching services. A proxy server works as a gateway that separates a network from an outside network and as a firewall that protects the network from an outside intrusion.

RADIUS logs: Remote Authentication Dial-In User Service is a method of authenticating remote users connecting to a network. The logs of a RADIUS server will provide the Internet Protocol address or phone number of the user requesting authentication to the network.

Redirector: A device or command used to forward or route Internet traffic to another Internet Protocol address; sometimes used to obscure the source or destination address.

Router: A device that determines the next network point to which a data packet should be forwarded to reach its destination. The router is connected to at least two networks and determines which way to send each data packet based on its current understanding of the state of the networks it is connected to.

Server: A computer that provides files and services for use by other computers.

Sniffer: Software that monitors network packets and can be used to intercept data including passwords, credit card numbers, etc.

Spoof: To change the identifying information in a communication in order to hide one's true identity.

Telnet: An Internet Protocol application for initiating a remote terminal session on a network.

Threads: Groups of associated messages and responses in message boards or newsgroups.

Trojan: An application that overtly does one thing while covertly doing another.

UTC: UTC has no direct word association. It means both Coordinated Universal Time in English and Temps Universel Coordonné in French. Coordinated Universal Time is the new worldwide time standard based on highly accurate atomic time and used in place of Greenwich Mean Time (GMT). UTC, like GMT, is set at 0 degrees longitude on the prime meridian.

Virus: A malicious application that by design spreads from one computer to another.

Wayback Machine: A historical archive of World Wide Web content located at www.archive.org.

Worm: A type of virus that self-replicates across a network.

Appendix B. Domain Name Extensions

- .aero (restricted to certain members of the global aviation community), sponsored by Societe Internationale de Telecommunications Aeronautiques SC (SITA).

- .biz (restricted to businesses), operated by NeuLevel.

- .com, operated by Verisign Global Registry Services.

- .coop (restricted to cooperatives), sponsored by Dot Cooperation LLC.

- .info, operated by Afilias Limited.

- .museum (restricted to museums and related persons), sponsored by the Museum Domain Management Association (MuseDoma).

- .name (restricted to individuals), operated by Global Name Registry.

- .net, operated by Verisign Global Registry Services.

- .org, operated by Public Interest Registry.

- .pro (restricted to licensed professionals), operated by RegistryPro.

Registrar contact information and descriptions are available at http://www.icann.org/registrars/accreditation-qualified-list.html.

Appendix C. Accessing Detailed Headers in E-Mail Messages

E-Mail Client Software	Display Detailed Header Information
AOL®	Select **Mail**, select **Mail Settings**, select **Advanced**, then select **Never Minimize Headers.**
Claris Emailer®	Under **Mail**, select **Show Long Headers.**
Eudora® (before ver. 3x)	Select **Tools**, select **Options**, select **Fonts & Display**, then select **Show all headers.**
Eudora® (ver. 3.x to ver. 6x IBM® or Macintosh®)	Select **BLAH, BLAH, BLAH** button on the incoming mail message.
GroupWise®	Click **"actions" and "delivery."**
HotMail®	Select **Options** on the Hotmail® Navigation Bar on the left side of the page. On the Options page, select **Preferences.** Scroll down to **Message Headers,** and select **Full.**
Lotus Notes® 4.6.x	From the menu bar, select **Actions**, then select **Delivery Information.**
Lotus Notes® R5	From the menu bar, select **Actions,** select **Tools,** then select **Delivery Information.**
Netscape® 4.xx	Double click on the e-mail message. Select **View Headers,** then select **All.**
Outlook®	Double click on the e-mail in your inbox to open the message. Select **View,** then select **Options.**
Outlook Express®	Open the e-mail message. From the File drop-down menu, select **Properties,** then select the **Details** tab.
PINE	Turn on the header option in setup, then type "h" to get headers.

Some e-mail clients do not comply with any Internet standards (e.g., cc-Mail, Beyond Mail, VAX VMS) and therefore do not maintain detailed header information. It will not be possible to obtain detailed headers from these e-mail messages.

When investigating e-mail messages sent over an intranet (internal network), know that in many cases e-mail headers are not generated. America Online (AOL) acts as an intranet for e-mail messages that are sent from one AOL member to another AOL member. These messages do not contain standard e-mail header information. However, an e-mail message ID may still be available.

Appendix D. File Sharing Investigative Suggested Checklist

Contraband files/data are present or criminal action took place

✓ Confirm jurisdiction.
✓ Identify the suspect.
✓ Identify any screen names and how they tie to the suspect.
✓ Identify the program used.
✓ Detail how the suspect was located.
✓ Determine if any exculpatory evidence is present (Trojan, virus, etc.).
✓ Review suspect statement/interview/confession.
✓ Use traditional investigative methods and procedures.
✓ Establish intent.
✓ Consult expert if necessary.

Online considerations

✓ Account names/number.
✓ Host information.
✓ Passwords.
✓ Channel/room.
✓ Was FTP site active—IP routable.
✓ Service being used.

Documentation

✓ Timelines.
✓ Chain of custody—logs/files.
✓ Summary.
✓ Glossary.
✓ Visual aids.
✓ Background of suspect on Internet.
✓ Good notes at each step of the investigation.
✓ Appendix of evidence.
✓ Photos/screen prints.

Appendix E. Sample Subpoenas and Reports

Sample 1: Subpoena for Documents When Probable Cause Is Required by State Law

STATE OF WISCONSIN)

COUNTY OF _____)

               S.S.

THE STATE OF WISCONSIN TO:
Internet Service Provider
Attn: Legal Compliance Department
Address
City, State, Zip Code

Pursuant to Wisconsin Statutes Section 968.135, upon request of the District Attorney and upon a showing of probable cause, you are hereby commanded to produce to the issuing court on _____, 2005, at _____ AM/PM, *or in lieu of appearing in court*, to make arrangements to deliver same to Detective _____ of the _____ Police Department (Fax xxx-xxx-xxxx) prior to that date, copies of the following records:

1. All customer or subscriber account information for the e-mail accounts hacker@suspect.net and suspect@hacker.net and also any accounts registered to Suspect, <u>date of birth.</u> For each such account the information shall include:

    a. The subscriber's name;

    b. The subscriber's address;

    c. The subscriber's telephone number or numbers, the e-mail address or addresses, account or login name or names, and any other information pertaining to the identity of the subscriber, including any identification numbers or credit card numbers or any other identifying information regarding the subscriber; and

    d. The types of services subscribed to or utilized by the subscriber and the lengths of such services.

2. The content of electronic communications not in "electronic storage" (i.e., any and all electronic mail that has already been opened by the user) currently held or maintained in the account associated with the address hacker@suspect.net and suspect@hacker.net and also any other accounts registered to Suspect, sent from or to the above account(s) during the period of November 2004 up through and including the date of this subpoena.

3. The content of all electronic communications in "electronic storage" for more than 180 days associated with the accounts identified above that were placed or stored in **ISP** computer systems in directories or files owned or controlled by such accounts at any time up through and including the date of this subpoena. **ISP** should NOT produce any unopened incoming electronic communications (i.e., electronic communications in "electronic storage") that are less than 181 days old.

Failure to comply with this subpoena may result in punishment for contempt under Chapter 785 of the Wisconsin Statutes.

Given under my hand the 19th day of July, 2005

BY THE COURT:

_____

Judge

Sample 2: Subpoena for Documents When Probable Cause Is Not Required Under State Law

IN THE CIRCUIT COURT OF THE NINTH JUDICIAL CIRCUIT
IN AND FOR ORANGE COUNTY, FLORIDA

IN RE: STATEWIDE PROSECUTOR: OSWP No.: 2005–0091–CFB
CRIMINAL INVESTIGATION: Subpoena No.: 05–165

INVESTIGATIVE SUBPOENA DUCES TECUM

IN THE NAME OF THE STATE OF FLORIDA, TO ALL AND SINGULAR THE AGENTS OF THE FLORIDA DEPARTMENT OF LAW ENFORCEMENT AND/OR THE SHERIFFS OF THE STATE OF FLORIDA.

YOU ARE COMMANDED TO SUMMON:

ISP Provider
Attn: _____
Address
City, State Zip Code

to appear before the undersigned Assistant Statewide Prosecutor on the ___ day of _____, 2005 at 1 p.m. at the Office of Statewide Prosecution, Central Florida Bureau, 135 W. Central Blvd., Suite 1000, Orlando, FL 32801, to testify truthfully in behalf of the State of Florida, and to bring with her the following items:

Please provide us with the information of who was assigned the IP address 205.188.197.57 on 05–31–05 at 12:06 AM (EST).

This SUBPOENA is issued under the authority of the Circuit Court, at the request of the Office of Statewide Prosecution, by and through the undersigned prosecuting attorney. Failure to obey this Order may be punished as contempt of court.

In lieu of personal appearance, these items may be furnished on or before the above date by **mail or personal delivery to:**

Chad Hanging
Assistant Statewide Prosecutor
135 W. Central Boulevard, Suite 1000
Orlando, FL 32801

This subpoena is issued as part of an ongoing criminal investigation. Do not disclose the existence of this subpoena or the State's investigation to (YOUR CUSTOMERS, SUBSCRIBERS, ETC.).

IN WITNESS WHEREOF, I have set my hand hereunto, and the seal of the Court at Orlando, Florida, this_____day of May, 2005.

_____
CLERK OF THE CIRCUIT COURT

BY: _____(Seal)
   Deputy Clerk
   Clerk of the Circuit Court

[Name]
Statewide Prosecutor

BY:

   Chad Hanging
   Assistant Statewide Prosecutor
   28 West Central Boulevard, Suite 300
   Orlando, FL 32801
   407–555–0893

Personally served this _____ day of May, 2005

By: _____

In accordance with the Americans With Disabilities Act, persons with a disability who need special accommodations to participate in this proceeding should contact _____, Assistant Statewide Prosecutor, not later than 10 days prior to the proceeding.

Sample 3: E-Mail Investigation Report

_____ **POLICE DEPARTMENT**

Date of Report:	3/26/2003	**Case No:**	2003–0326–1750
		Ref. No:	
Occurred Incident:	21 – Fraud	**Sec/Area:**	ABC/CENTRAL
Dispatched as:	21 – Fraud	**Grid:**	CAPITOL

Case Offense: **FRAUD**
Addr of Occurrence: 316 Main St.
Call Date/Time: 03/07/2003 09:24   **From Date/Time**:
Dispatch Date/Time: 03/07/2003 09:25   **Thru Date/Time:**
Reporting Officer: DET JOE FRIDAY
Special Routing:

SUSPECT **JOHN DOE, III**
M/W, DOB: 11/22/74 (28 yrs) Height: 6'1" Weight: 175
123 WILSON ST., ANYTOWN
C: 555-7789
ID: BY CALIFORNIA ID CARD

VICTIM **JANE SMITH**
F/W DOB: 11/05/76 (26 yrs)
316 Main St. H: 555-5854
EMPLOYER: XYZ Inc. IN WASHINGTON, D.C.
SCHOOL: 3RD YEAR LAW STUDENT

CONTACT: **POLLY COTTON**
INTERNET ASSIGNED NUMBERS AUTHORITY
PH: 555–9358

CONTACT: **MILT BRADLEY**
CABLE COMMUNICATIONS, INTERNET SECURITY
PH: 555–5754

On 3/19/03, John Doe forwarded the following e-mail to me, advising that it was evidence that Jane Smith had given him permission to use her First Federal checking account. He told me that he had received the e-mail from Jane, and that he had forwarded it to several of his e-mail accounts to preserve it.

After reviewing the e-mail, I was skeptical that it had come from Smith, due to the odd content, which seemed directed at deflecting responsibility from Doe. I advised Doe that I had experience in computer-related investigations, and that I intended to trace the e-mail to its origin, to confirm or deny his claim that the e-mail had originated from Smith. I advised him that if the e-mail had been created by him and "spoofed" to appear that it was from her, in order to alter the course of my investigation, further charges could result. He advised that he understood this, and told me, "It came from her."

The content of the e-mail is as follows. The IP addresses the mail was routed through have been highlighted for readability:

Return-Path: <jsmith@coolmale.com>
Received: from rly-xe02.mx.lol.com (rly-xe02.mail.lol.com [172.xx.xxx.xxx]) by air-xe05.mail.lol.com (v90_r2.5) with ESMTP id MAILINXE54-0307124425; Fri, 07 Mar 2003 12:44:25 -0500
Received: from coolmale.com (f18.law11.coolmale.com [64.x.xx.18]) by rly-xe02.mx.lol.com (v92.16) with ESMTP id MAILRELAYINXE23-4133e68da602e0; Fri, 07 Mar 2003 12:44:00 -0500
Received: from mail pickup service by coolmale.com with Microsoft SMTPSVC;
        Fri, 7 Mar 2003 09:43:59 -0800
Received: from 66.xx.xx.62 by lw11fd.law11.coolmale.com with HTTP;
        Fri, 07 Mar 2003 17:43:58 GMT
X-Originating-IP: [66.xx.xx.62]
From: "JaneSmith" <jsmith@coolmale.com>
To: jdoe@lol.com
Date: Fri, 07 Mar 2003 12:43:58 -0500
Mime-Version: 1.0
Content-Type: text/html
Message-ID: <F18EOXS7YN38CfCsvCs0000371d@coolmale.com>
X-OriginalArrivalTime: 07 Mar 2003 17:43:59.0916 (UTC)
FILETIME=[22931EC0:01C2E4D1]
X-Mailer: Unknown (No Version)

John

I am sorry that I had to take these actions against you but you left me no choice. I know I gave you my permission to endorse,deposit,and withdrawl from my check-ing account. But I wasn't aware that you would turn into such a different person. I don't know you anymore. The only reason I turned you in was to get back at you for [expletive] me over emotionally. If you would have treated me with the slightest amount of kindness I would have just let things be. This is my turn to make you feel like [expletive] and if you go to jail because of it so be it. I know you thought that I wouldn't do anything considering you had my permission but I think you need to feel what I have. I never want to see you again.

Jane

I began tracing the e-mail via IP addresses contained in the header portion, starting with the bottom (which corresponds with the recipient's IP) and moving toward the top (which corresponds with the sender's IP). Using the Internet tracing tools at Geektools.com, I discovered the following:

- 66.xx.xx.62 by lw11fd.law11.coolmale.com is registered to Cable Communications.

- f18.law11.coolmale.com [64.x.xx.18] is registered to Coolmale.

- rly-xe02.mail.lol.com [172.xx.xxx.xxx] is registered to the Internet Assigned Numbers Authority (IANA) as part of a "Special Purpose" block of IP addresses.

On 3/25/03 at 11:30 a.m., I contacted Polly Cotton, Security Specialist for IANA to inquire about what the "special purpose" block of addresses was, and who it was assigned to so that I could follow up on the origin of the e-mail from that point. She advised me that the IANA assigns blocks of Internet addresses to Internet service providers and others all over the world. She further advised that a small portion of the IP addresses on the Internet are designated as "special purpose," and that the purpose of these addresses vary.

I provided Polly Cotton with the IP address in question, 172.xx.xxx.xxx, and she was able to advise that this address belonged to a group of IPs known as "Private use addresses." Cotton informed me that Private Use Addresses are intended for private Intranet (internal networks) use only, and are not publicly available.

She advised that these addresses are commonly used for forged e-mails, as they cannot be traced to any individual user, only to the entity that the block of IP numbers is assigned to.

Cotton told me that private use address blocks are commonly assigned to Cable and Broadband Internet service providers for their internal use, and that the number should not have been available publicly. She was able to confirm that the block of IP addresses that included 172.xx.xxx.xxx was assigned to Cable Communications, and suggested that I contact them for further information about how this IP could have been accessed and used.

Contact with Cable Communications:

I next contacted Milt Bradley, an Internet Security Specialist with Cable Communications. I explained the situation to him, and he confirmed that Cable holds the private use IP 172.xx.xxx.xxx. He advised that the only way this number would have legitimately showed up in an e-mail from Smith to Doe is if both the sender and receiver were work-ing from machines with Cable pipeline service and cable modems. He told me that if the alleged sender didn't have Cable pipeline service at the computer the e-mail was sent from, she didn't send the e-mail. He advised me that more likely, the originating informa-tion was spoofed, or the sender accessed the coolmale account the message was sent from, and sent the message to the same computer the message was received at.

Contact with Jane Smith:

On 3/25/03, I spoke in person with Jane Smith at the CCB detective bureau at approxi-mately 2 p.m. I asked her about her Internet service, and she advised that she has dial-up service through the Internet Service Provider LOL at her house, and occasionally uses the university computers to check and send e-mail. I asked her more specifically about her whereabouts on 3/7/03, at the time the e-mail was sent. After looking at the calendar, she advised that she would have been in class or between classes, and that any e-mail she sent would have been from the university system. I asked her if she had any friends with cable modem access to the Internet or who use Cable Communications as an ISP, and she advised that she did not that she was aware of.

I allowed Smith to review the e-mail forwarded to me by Doe, and she told me, "I didn't write that." She then told me, "Oh, my god. He's got access to my e-mail account." She explained that she had given Doe her e-mail password so that he could forward documents received at that e-mail address to her in Virginia while she was working there.

Smith advised me that she has four e-mail accounts, jsmith@coolmale.com with a password of 'plado', jsmith@lol.com with a password of 'badger1', jane.smith@xyzinc.com with a password of 'badger4', and jsmith@university.edu with a password she doesn't remember, as she forwards all mail from there to her personal e-mail address. She told me at that point she suspected that Doe had accessed her e-mail account to send the message to himself, to make it appear as if it had come from her.

Smith also told me that the verbiage of the e-mail seemed to be in his voice. She told me that comments in the e-mail such as "[expletive] me over emotionally" and "This is my turn to make you feel like [expletive]" seemed to her to be "his voice." She also told me that she is a "punctuation and grammar nazi" and would never misspell the word withdrawal, or leave out the spaces after the commas behind the words endorse, deposit, and withdrawal. She also told me that the e-mail was dated after the time she had reported the fraudulent activity to the police and had told John she was doing so, and she felt he was trying to undermine her credibility.

Smith admitted to me that she had written some nasty things to John over e-mail and via instant messaging, but that this e-mail was definitely not from her. She then told me, "Why would I file a report to the police saying he didn't have my permission to do this and then write an e-mail to him saying 'I know I gave you my permission to endorse, deposit, and withdrawal from my checking account.' That's just stupid."

Investigation continuing.

Supervisory Officer: _____ I.D.: _____

Reporting Officer: _____ I.D.: _____
                        DETECTIVE JOE FRIDAY

Sample 4: United States Secret Service (USSS) Memorandum Report

From: SAIC – Los Angeles Field Office

To: SAIC – Criminal Investigative Division

                        RAIC – London Resident Office

Info: Electronic Crimes Task Forces

Origin: Field

Office: Los Angeles Field Office

Case Number: 403–775–xxxxxx–s

Case Title: Internet Worm

Case Type: 775.310 Unauthorized Computer Access That Adversely Affects Operations

Actual/Potential Loss: Unknown/Unknown

Status: Continued

Synopsis:

On 01/03/2005, a self-replicating computer worm, called "Internet Worm," was found on several computer servers belonging to the local county Information Technology Department. This worm has also infected thousands of machines across the globe by spreading itself through a known vulnerability in a "server operating system." Each client then attempts to report back to several central Internet Relay Chat (IRC) servers.

Two suspects have been identified, one in the United Kingdom and one in Texas.

Search warrants are being prepared in both cases, which will be executed simultaneously.

Case continued pending further investigation.

Details of investigation:

On 01/03/2005, the local county Information Technology Security Officer (ITSO) in "Any Town USA" contacted the City Police Department and advised that they had found unauthorized software on three computers belonging to the county Information Technology Department. An investigator from the City Police responded and took custody of the three computers. The investigator contacted Special Agent "MANN," from the local U.S. Secret Service, who was able to respond in order to assist in a computerized forensic examination.

Subsequent forensic examinations were conducted on the three computers, which revealed that all three were compromised by a source originating outside of the county network. An electronic "worm" had exploited a known vulnerability in the operating system, which the system manufacturer was aware of and attempted to address by releasing a "patch" for this vulnerability back in June 2004.

The worm operates by first finding an unpatched server, which is currently running, and then infecting the machine by copying its exploitation toolkit to the machine. The following domain names are coded into the configuration files of the worm:

-badguy.badguynet.uk
-badguy1.badguynet.uk
-badguy2.badguynet.uk

These domain names are dynamic and permit the perpetrators to change computers/machines.

The worm attempts to connect to one of the three "Internet Relay Chat" (IRC) servers, which are pointed to by the domain names. IRC is a software program that allows users to connect to a central server located anywhere on the Internet and chat with other users, who are connected to that server or any other linked server that is linked together. Chat servers can have hundreds of users and allow almost an unlimited number of "channels" or "chat rooms." Each chat room or channel is typically created with a separate topic or theme. Chat rooms are controlled by the first user into the channel and are designated as "channel operators." Channel operators can kick people out of the chat rooms, ban users, moderate discussions, and password protect the chat room so only people who know the password can enter the channel.

Once a compromised computer enters the password-protected chat room on one of these servers, it then sits idle waiting for various commands that a suspect/perpetrator might type in the chat room. These commands will cause the compromised computer to perform a preprogrammed function, such as: delete a file; copy a file; send a file to the channel operator; display information about the system; or even start and stop programs on the computer. The worm will then create a "bounce proxy" service on the victim machine. This proxy will permit the suspect to reroute network traffic through the victim machine, allowing the suspect/perpetrator to communicate with any computer on the network and making it appear that the network traffic is originating from the victim's computer.

Furthermore, the worm will start to randomly scan the Internet for more vulnerable servers to infect, and the process will be repeated over and over.

With this information, and continuing on 01/03/05, Special Agent MANN connected to the badguy.badguy.uk IRC server and observed a welcome screen that said "Internet Worm Home." The Agent was automatically entered into the chat room and he witnessed several hundred other victim machines connected to the server, waiting for commands from the suspect(s).

Special Agent MANN determined that the domain name "badguy.uk" is owned and operated by a company named Badguy Dynamic Network Services (BGDNS), located in Anycity, USA. The company operates a domain "pointing" service that allows users to register their home or business computer(s), which permits them to receive incoming connections from the Internet based on a domain name. For example, when someone connects to badguy2.badguy.uk, they are initially connected to badguy.uk servers; but they are also immediately redirected to the address associated with badguy2. The badguy.uk company will have to know the Internet Protocol (IP) address, which is the unique number of that person's home or business computer, in order to "point" that domain name to their computer.

Special Agent MANN contacted BGDNS, and their director of security and personnel agreed to cooperate with this investigation. BGDNS advised that one of the domain names used by the suspects to run the IRC servers, which the compromised computers connect to, is "badguy2.badguy.uk." Badguy.uk provided the registration information concerning this domain name to include the e-mail address used by the suspect(s) when they registered for the service, hacker@suspect.net.

On 01/03/05, Special Agent MANN conducted a standard Internet search using a search engine and found five (5) related newsgroup messages that referenced the e-mail address of hacker@suspect.net. All the newsgroup messages were advertising computer-related items that he/she was selling on an Internet auction service. Three of the five ended the posting with the tag "==hack==." The messages were posted by the unique IP address XXX.XXX.XXX.XXX within a few minutes of each other on July 20, 2004, indicating that they were written by the same person.

On 01/06/05, Special Agent MANN contacted an investigator with the Internet auction service. The investigator was able to identify a unique account from the two newsgroup postings by examining the message that advertised the items. By taking the item number, the investigator was able to identify an account that uses the e-mail address of suspect@hacker.net. The investigator was also able to determine that the person who registered this account resides at 10 Main Street, Anytown, United Kingdom. Special Agent MANN was able to obtain three credit card numbers that were provided by the suspect when he registered for the auction account. All three credit cards were issued by "Bank of Anytown UK" and were issued in the name of suspect.

On 01/07/05, Special Agent MANN also conducted a standard Internet search using an Internet search engine, which revealed approximately 50 newsgroup messages posted by the e-mail address suspect@hacker.net. Several of the messages were about hacking and breaking into computer systems. Agent MANN then used publicly available Internet tools to look up the domain registration information related to hacker.net, and found that the domain name had been registered with fraudulent information.

On 01/12/2005, Agent MANN was able to register the domain name badguy1.badguy.uk. This domain name was previously used by the suspect and is programmed into the Internet Worm as one of the IRC servers. The suspect had previously registered this domain name on a 30-day trial basis, which has since expired; but the domain name was again available for anyone to utilize. Agent MANN signed up for the same free-trial service and pointed the domain to a USSS Los Angeles Electronic Crimes Task Force (LAECTF) computer operating in an undercover capacity. In a 12-hour period, the undercover computer was contacted by over 5,100 computers, which attempted to connect to the IRC server and the preprogrammed chat rooms.

Several hundred of these computers are owned and operated by various universities and technology companies throughout the world, and many belong to critical infrastructure programs, such as telecommunication companies, educational organizations, and commercial entities. The number of computers compromised has the potential risk of allowing the suspect(s) to initiate a severe "Distributed Denial of Service" (DDOS) attack because the suspect(s) has the ability to direct each compromised computer to send communication packets to a specific target computer anywhere on the Internet. This would cause the targeted computer to overload with communication requests and cause it to malfunction.

On 01/23/05, BGDNS was able to record the IP addresses that the suspect(s) used to connect to his Web site, in order to change where the domain names pointed. In the previous 2 days, a subject with the login name "hacker" changed 2 domain names for a total of 11 times. With each change, the network connection came from IP address YYY.YYY.YYY.YYY.

On 01/24/05, "Company Internet Provide" complied with a grand jury subpoena and informed Special Agent MANN that IP address YYY.YYY.YYY.YYY was assigned to customer "Suspect 2," located at 211 Main Street, Southtown, Texas. The Internet Provider also stated that this account was a residential account, with broadband access.

On 01/27/05, Agent MANN contacted the USSS Dallas Electronic Crimes Task Force (DECTF), and informed them about the information relating to Suspect 2. The DECTF stated that it would prepare a pen register/trap and trace court order to be executed on Suspect 2's broadband connection. The DECTF was further requested to explore the possibility of installing a "packet sniffer" at the Internet Provider's facilities, in order to capture packet headers on the suspect's Internet account.

On 01/29/05, the Internet Provider agreed to allow the USSS to connect a USSS computer to its switch in Dallas. The port on the switch will be configured by the Internet Provider to monitor all Internet traffic passing to or from the Suspect 2 broadband account.

In accordance with a pen register/trap and trace court order, the network monitoring computer will only capture Internet packet headers, to include the origin and destination IP address and ports. The content or payload of the packets will not be captured or recorded. The court order will be valid for 60 days from the date issued. Network monitoring will begin as soon as possible and will continue until the court order expires or notification is given by the Case Agent that the monitor is no longer needed.

Disposition:
Case continued pending further investigation.

Appendix F. Examples of Potential Sources of Evidence in Network Investigations (may be applied to other investigations)

Location	Potential source	What you might find	Who to ask first
Victim computer	<ul><li>Operating system logs</li><li>Application logs</li><li>Security logs</li><li>.ini files</li><li>Contraband files</li></ul>	<ul><li>Date and time stamps</li><li>User names and passwords</li><li>Connection information</li><li>IP addresses</li><li>Node names</li></ul>	<ul><li>Victim</li><li>Network administrator or installer</li></ul>
Victim-side firewall or router, Syslog server	<ul><li>Firewall logs</li><li>DHCP logs</li><li>NAT/PAT logs</li><li>Proxy logs</li></ul>	<ul><li>Address translations</li><li>Date and time stamps</li><li>User names and passwords</li><li>Connection information</li><li>IP addresses</li><li>Node names</li></ul>	<ul><li>Victim</li><li>Network administrator or installer</li></ul>
Victim ISP	<ul><li>Firewall logs</li><li>DHCP logs</li><li>NAT/PAT logs</li><li>Proxy logs</li></ul>		<ul><li>Victim ISP</li></ul>
Source ISP	<ul><li>Firewall logs</li><li>DHCP logs</li><li>NAT/PAT logs</li><li>Proxy logs</li></ul>		<ul><li>Source ISP</li></ul>
Source-side firewall, router, Syslog server	<ul><li>Firewall logs</li><li>DHCP logs</li><li>NAT/PAT logs</li><li>Proxy logs</li></ul>		<ul><li>Owner</li><li>Operator</li><li>Network administrator</li></ul>
Source computer	<ul><li>Operating system logs</li><li>Application logs</li><li>Security logs</li><li>.ini files</li><li>Contraband files</li></ul>	<ul><li>Date and time stamps</li><li>User names and passwords</li><li>Connection information</li><li>IP addresses</li><li>Node names</li></ul>	<ul><li>Owner</li><li>Operator</li><li>Network administrator</li></ul>

Appendix G. Sample Language for Preservation Request Letters Under 18 U.S.C. § 2703(f)

[Internet Service Provider]
[Address]

VIA FAX to (xxx) xxx-xxxx

Dear:

I am writing to [confirm our telephone conversation earlier today and to] make a formal request for the preservation of records and other evidence pursuant to 18 U.S.C. § 2703(f) pending further legal process.

You are hereby requested to preserve, for a period of 90 days, the records described below currently in your possession, including records stored on backup media, in a form that includes the complete record. You also are requested not to disclose the existence of this request to the subscriber or any other person, other than as necessary to comply with this request. **If compliance with this request may result in a permanent or temporary termination of service to the accounts described below, or otherwise alert the subscriber or user of these accounts as to your actions to preserve the referenced files and records, please contact me before taking such actions.**

This request applies only retrospectively. It does not in any way obligate you, nor are you being asked, to capture and preserve new information that arises after the date of this request.

This preservation request applies to the following records and evidence:

A. All stored communications and other files reflecting communications to or from [E-mail Account/User name/IP Address or Domain Name (between DATE1 at TIME1 and DATE2 at TIME2)];

B. All files that have been accessed by [E-mail Account/User name/IP Address or Domain Name (between DATE1 at TIME1 and DATE2 at TIME2)] or are controlled by user accounts associated with [E-mail Account/User name/IP Address or Domain Name (between DATE1 at TIME1 and DATE2 at TIME2)];

C. All connection logs and records of user activity for [E-mail Account/User name/IP Address or Domain Name (between DATE1 at TIME1 and DATE2 at TIME2)], including:

1. Connection date and time;

2. Disconnect date and time;

3. Method of connection (e.g., Telnet, ftp, http);

4. Type of connection (e.g., modem, cable/DSL, T1/LAN);

5. Data transfer volume;

6. User name associated with the connection and other connection information, including the Internet Protocol address of the source of the connection;

7. Telephone caller identification records;

8. Records of files or system attributes accessed, modified, or added by the user;

9. Connection information for other computers to which the user of the [E-mail Account/User name/IP Address or Domain Name (between DATE1 at TIME1 and DATE2 at TIME2)] connected, by any means, during the connection period, including the destination IP address, connection time and date, disconnect time and date, method of connection to the destination computer, the identities (account and screen names) and subscriber information, if known, for any person or entity to which such connection information relates, and all other information related to the connection from ISP or its subsidiaries.

All records and other evidence relating to the subscriber(s), customer(s), account holder(s), or other entity(ies) associated with [E-mail Account/User name/IP Address or Domain Name (between DATE1 at TIME1 and DATE2 at TIME2)], including, without limitation, subscriber names, user names, screen names or other identities, mailing addresses, residential addresses, business addresses, e-mail addresses and other contact information, telephone numbers or other subscriber number or identifier number, billing records, information about the length of service and the types of services the subscriber or customer utilized, and any other identifying information, whether such records or other evidence are in electronic or other form.

Any other records and other evidence relating to [E-mail Account/User name/IP Address or Domain Name (between DATE1 at TIME1 and DATE2 at TIME2)]. Such records and other evidence include, without limitation, correspondence and other records of contact by any person or entity about the above-referenced account, the content and connection logs associated with or relating to postings, and communications and any other activities to or through [E-mail Account/User name/IP Address or Domain Name (between DATE1 at TIME1 and DATE2 at TIME2)], whether such records or other evidence are in electronic or other form.

Very truly yours,

Signature _____

Printed Name _____

Title_____

Appendix H. Sample Language for 2703(d) Court Order and Application

IN THE CIRCUIT COURT FOR THE ****** JUDICIAL CIRCUIT
IN AND FOR ***** COUNTY, FLORIDA

STATE OF FLORIDA   CASE NO:

vs.

Defendant

_____/

APPLICATION

COMES NOW the State of Florida, by and through the undersigned Assistant Statewide Prosecutor, and hereby files, under seal, this *ex parte* application for an order pursuant to 18 USC §2703(d) to require [Internet Service Provider], [address], to provide records and other information pertaining to the [Internet Service Provider] account that was assigned Internet Protocol address xxx.xxx.xxx.xxx on [date] and [time] est.

FACTUAL BACKGROUND

[Insert factual background here – probable cause]

LEGAL BACKGROUND

18 U.S.C. § 2703 sets out particular requirements that the state must meet in order to obtain access to the records and other information in the possession of providers of "electronic communications services" and/or "remote computing services." [Internet Service Provider] functions both as an electronic communications service provider—that is, it provides its subscribers access to electronic communication services, including e-mail and the Internet—and as a remote computing service provider—it provides computer facilities for the storage and processing of electronic communications—as those terms are used in 18 U.S.C. § 2703. **[Note that because a "remote computing service" is public by definition, this statement must be modified if you are seeking information from a service provider who is not a provider to the public, such as, for example, a university.]**

Here, the state seeks to obtain three categories of records: (1) basic subscriber information; (2) records and other information, including connection logs, pertaining to certain subscribers; and **[Add only if the application seeks to obtain the contents of communications (such as e-mails) pursuant to § 2703(b), as opposed to mere records**

pursuant to § 2703(c).] (3) the content of electronic communications in a remote computing service (but not communications in electronic storage[20]).

To obtain basic subscriber information, such as the subscriber's name, address, billing information, and other identifying records, the state needs only a subpoena; however, the state may also compel such information through an order issued pursuant to section 2703(d). <u>See</u> 18 U.S.C. § 2703(c)(1)(C). To obtain other types of records and information pertaining to the subscribers or customers of service providers, including connection logs and other audit information, the state must comply with the dictates of sections 2703(c)(1)(B) and 2703(d). Section § 2703(c)(1)(B) provides in pertinent part:

> A provider of electronic communication service or remote computing service shall disclose a record or other information pertaining to a subscriber to or customer of such service (not including the contents of communications covered by subsection (a) or (b) of this section) to a governmental entity only when the governmental entity . . . obtains a court order for such disclosure under subsection (d) of this section;

[Add only if the application seeks to obtain the contents of communications (such as e-mails) pursuant to § 2703(b), as opposed to mere records pursuant to § 2703(c).] To obtain the contents of electronic communications held by a remote computing service (but not the contents in "electronic storage," <u>see</u> n.1), the state must comply with 2703(b)(1)(B), which provides, in pertinent part:

> A governmental entity may require a provider of remote computing service to disclose the contents of any electronic communication to which this paragraph is made applicable by paragraph 2 of this subsection . . . with prior notice from the state entity to the subscriber or customer if the governmental entity . . . obtains a court order for such disclosure under subsection (d) of this section . . . . except that delayed notice may be given pursuant to section 2705 of this title.
>
> Paragraph 2 of subsection 2703(b) applies with respect to any electronic communication that is held or maintained on a remote computing service—
>
> (A) on behalf of, and received by means of electronic transmission from (or created by means of computer processing of communications received by means of electronic transmission from), a subscriber or customer of such remote computing service; and
>
> (B) solely for the purpose of providing storage or computer processing services to such subscriber or customer, if the provider is not authorized to access the contents of any such communications for purposes of providing any services other than storage or computer processing.

Therefore, communications described by paragraph 2 of subsection 2703(b) include the content of electronic mail that has been opened, viewed, downloaded, or otherwise accessed by the recipient and is held remotely by the service provider on its computers.

---

[20] "Electronic storage" is a term of art, specifically defined in 18 U.S.C. § 2510(17) as "(A) any temporary, intermediate storage of a wire or electronic communication incidental to the electronic transmission thereof; and (B) any storage of such communication by an electronic communication service for purposes of backup protection of such communication." The state does not seek access to any such materials.

All of the information the state seeks from [Internet Service Provider] through this application may be compelled through an order that complies with section 2703(d). Section 2703(d) provides in pertinent part:

> A court order for disclosure under subsection (b) or (c) may be issued by any court that is a court of competent jurisdiction described in section 3127(2)(A)[21] and shall issue only if the governmental entity offers specific and articulable facts showing that there are reasonable grounds to believe that the . . . records or other information sought, are relevant and material to an ongoing criminal investigation. . . . A court issuing an order pursuant to this section, on a motion made promptly by the service provider, may quash or modify such order, if the information or records requested are unusually voluminous in nature or compliance with such order otherwise would cause an undue burden on such provider.

Accordingly, this application sets forth facts showing there are reasonable grounds to believe that the materials sought are relevant and material to the ongoing criminal investigation.

REQUESTED INFORMATION

The state requests that [Internet Service Provider] be directed to produce all records described in Attachment 1 to this Application. This information is directly relevant to identifying the individual(s) responsible for the crime under investigation. The information requested should be readily accessible to [Internet Service Provider] by computer search, and its production should not prove to be unduly burdensome. **[Undersigned should check with the ISP before filing this document to ensure the accuracy of this statement.]**

The state requests that this Application and Order be sealed by the Court until such time as the court directs otherwise.

The State of Florida further requests that pursuant to the preclusion of notice provisions of 18 U.S.C. § 2705(b), that [Internet Service Provider] be ordered not to notify any person (including the subscriber or customer to which the materials relate) of the existence of this order for such period as the court deems appropriate. The State of Florida submits that such an order is justified because notification of the existence of this order could seriously jeopardize the ongoing investigation. Such a disclosure could give the subscriber an opportunity to destroy evidence, notify confederates, or flee or continue his flight from prosecution.

[Add only if the application seeks to obtain the contents of communications pursuant to § 2703(b), as opposed to mere records pursuant to § 2703(c).] The State of Florida further requests, pursuant to the delayed notice provisions of 18 U.S.C. § 2705(a), an order delaying any notification to the subscriber or customer that may be required by § 2703(b) to obtain the contents of communications, for a period of 90 days. Providing prior notice to the subscriber or customer could seriously jeopardize the ongoing investigation, as such a disclosure would give the subscriber an opportunity to destroy evidence, change patterns of behavior, notify confederates, or flee or continue his flight from prosecution. **[Optional Baker Act language to use if the ISP is a university: The State of Florida further requests that [Internet Service Provider]'s compliance with**

---

[21] 18 USC § 3127(2) defines the term "court of competent jurisdiction" as "(A) any district court of the United States (including a magistrate judge of such a court) or any United States court of appeals having jurisdiction over the offense being investigated; or (B) a court of general criminal jurisdiction of a State authorized by the law of that State to enter orders authorizing the use of a pen register or a trap and trace device." Because 18 USC § 2703(d) expressly permits "any" such court to issue an order, this court may enter an order directing the disclosure of such information even if the information is stored outside of this judicial circuit.

the delayed notification provisions of this Order shall be deemed authorized under 20 U.S.C. § 1232g(b)(1)(j)(ii) (the "Baker Act"). See 34 CFR § 99.31(a)(9)(i) (exempting requirement of prior notice for disclosures made to comply with a judicial order or lawfully issued subpoena where the disclosure is made pursuant to "any other subpoena issued for a law enforcement purpose and the court or other issuing agency has ordered that the existence or the contents of the subpoena or the information furnished in response to the subpoena not be disclosed")].

WHEREFORE, it is respectfully requested that the Court grant the attached Order, (1) directing [Internet Service Provider] to provide the State of Florida with the records and information described in Attachment 1; (2) directing that the Application and Order be sealed; (3) directing [Internet Service Provider] not to disclose the existence or content of the Order, except to the extent necessary to carry out the Orders; and **[Use only if the application seeks to obtain the contents of communications pursuant to § 2703(b)]** (4) directing that the notification by the state otherwise required by 18 U.S.C. § 2703(b) be delayed for ninety days.

Respectfully Submitted,

_____

Assistant Statewide Prosecutor

ATTACHMENT 1

You are to provide the following information as printouts and as ASCII data files:

A. All customer or subscriber account information for any accounts registered to _____, or associated with _____ . For each such account, the information shall include:

1. The subscriber's account and login name(s);
2. The subscriber's address;
3. The subscriber's telephone number or numbers;
4. The subscriber's e-mail address;
5. Any other information pertaining to the identity of the subscriber, including, but not limited to billing information (including type and number of credit cards, student identification number, or other identifying information).

B. User connection logs for:

(1) all accounts identified in Part A, above,

(2) the IP address [xxx.xxx.xxx.xxx], for the time period beginning ____ through and including the date of this order, for any connections to or from ____.

User connection logs should contain the following:

1. Connection time and date;
2. Disconnect time and date;
3. Method of connection to system (e.g., SLIP, PPP, Shell);
4. Data transfer volume (e.g., bytes);
5. Connection information for other systems to which user connected via, including:
    a. Connection destination;
    b. Connection time and date;
    c. Disconnect time and date;
    d. Method of connection to system (e.g., Telnet, ftp, http);
    e. Data transfer volume (e.g., bytes).

C. **[Add only if the application seeks to obtain the contents of communications (such as e-mails) pursuant to § 2703(b), as opposed to mere records pursuant to § 2703(c).]** The contents of electronic communications (not in electronic storage[22]) that were placed or stored in directories or files owned or controlled by the accounts identified in Part A at any time after [date] up through and including the date of this Order.

---

[22] "Electronic storage" is a term of art, specifically defined in 18 U.S.C. § 2510(17) as "(A) any temporary, intermediate storage of a wire or electronic communication incidental to the electronic transmission thereof; and (B) any storage of such communication by an electronic communication service for purposes of backup protection of such communication." The government does not seek access to any such materials.

Appendix I. Technical Resources List

National resources

Bureau of Alcohol, Tobacco, Firearms and Explosives
www.atf.gov

National White Collar Crime Center
1000 Technology Drive, Suite 2130
Fairmont, WV 26554
Phone: 877–628–7674
http://www.nw3c.org

Office of Juvenile Justice and Delinquency Prevention Internet Crimes Against Children Program
810 Seventh Street N.W.
Washington, DC 20001
Phone: 202–616–7323
http://www.ojp.usdoj.gov/ojjdp

SEARCH Group, Inc.
The National Consortium for Justice
  Information and Statistics
7311 Greenhaven Drive, Suite 145
Sacramento, CA 95831
Phone: 916–392–2550
http://www.search.org

U.S. Department of Defense Cyber Crime Center
911 Elkridge Landing Road, Suite 300
Linthicum, MD 21090
Phone: 410–981–1627/877–981–3235
http://www.dc3.mil/dc3/home.htm

U.S. Department of Homeland Security Bureau of Immigration and Customs Enforcement Cyber Crimes Center (C3)
11320 Random Hills Road, Suite 400
Fairfax, VA 22030
Phone: 703–293–8005

U.S. Secret Service Electronic Crimes Task Force
http://www.ectaskforce.org/

Task Force Regional Locations

Bay Area Electronic Crimes Task Force
345 Spear Street
San Francisco, CA 94105
Phone: 415–744–9026
Fax: 415–744–9051

Chicago Electronic Crimes Task Force
525 West Van Buren
Chicago, IL 60607
Phone: 312–353–5431
Fax: 312–353–1225

Cleveland Electronic Crimes Task Force
6100 Rockside Woods Boulevard
Cleveland, OH 44131–2334
Phone: 216–706–4365
Fax: 216–706–4445

Dallas N-Tec Electronic Crimes Task Force
125 East John W. Carpenter
Irvine, TX 75062–2752
Phone: 972–868–3200

Houston HITEC Electronic Crimes Task Force
602 Sawyer Street
Houston, TX 77007
Phone: 713–868–2299
Fax: 713–868–5093

Las Vegas Electronic Crimes Task Force
600 Las Vegas Boulevard South, Suite 700
Las Vegas, NV 89101
Phone: 702–388–6571
Fax: 702–388–6668

Los Angeles Electronic Crimes Task Force
725 South Figueroa Street, 13th Floor
Los Angeles, CA 90017–5418
Phone: 213–894–4830
  (General Office for USSS)
Phone: 213–533–4650
  (Direct Phone for ECTF)

Metro-Charlotte Electronic/Financial Crimes Task Force
One Fairview Center
6302 Fairview Road
Charlotte, NC 28210
Phone: 704–442–8370
Fax: 704–442–8369

Miami Electronic Crimes Task Force
10350 N.W. 112 Avenue
Miami, Florida 33178
Phone: 305–863–5000

New England Electronic Crimes Task Force
Tip O'Neil Federal Building
10 Causeway Street, Room 791
Boston, MA 02222
Phone: 617–565–6640
Fax: 617–565–5659

New York Electronic Crimes Task Force
335 Adams Street, 32nd Floor
Brooklyn, NY 11201
Phone: 718–625–7135
Fax: 718–625–3919

South Carolina Electronic Crimes Task Force
107 Westpark Boulevard, Suite 301
Columbia, SC 29210
Phone: 803–772–4015

Washington-Metro Electronic Crimes Task Force
1100 L Street N.W.
Washington, DC 20003
Phone: 202–406–8000
Fax: 202–406–8803

State resources

The U.S. Department of Justice has created the **Computer and Telecommunication Coordinator (CTC) Program.** Each United States Attorney's Office (USAO) has designated at least one CTC. This list and contact information can be found at: http://www.cybercrime.gov/CTClist.htm.

The **American Prosecutors Research Institute (APRI)** is the research, training, and technical assistance affiliate of the National District Attorneys Association. The 50 State **Peer-to-Peer Technical Assistance Network (P2PTAN)** comprises State and local prosecutors who are involved in prosecuting high-tech and computer-related crime and has been compiled for use by law enforcement officers and prosecutors. This list and contact information can be found at: http://www.ndaa-apri.org/pdf/7_8_04_point_of_contact.pdf.

Alabama

Alabama Bureau of Investigation
Internet Crimes Against Children Unit
716 Arcadia Circle
Huntsville, AL 35801
Phone: 800–228–7688
E-mail: info@dps.state.al.us
http://www.dps.state.al.us/public/abi/icac/

Alabama Bureau of Investigation
3402 Demetropolis Road
Mobile, AL 36693
Phone: 251–660–2350
http://www.dps.state.al.us/public/abi/icac

Homewood Police Department
1833 29th Avenue South
Homewood, AL 35209
Phone: 205–877–8637

Hoover Police Department
FBI Innocent Images Task Force,
  Birmingham
100 Municipal Drive
Hoover, AL 35216
Phone: 205–444–7700

Office of the Attorney General
Public Corruption and White Collar
  Crime Division
11 South Union Street
Montgomery, AL 36130
Phone: 334–353–8494

Alaska

Alaska State Troopers
White Collar Crime Section
5700 East Tudor Road
Anchorage, AK 99507
Phone: 907–269–5627
http://www.dps.state.ak.us/ast/abi/
  WhiteCollar.asp

Anchorage Police Department
4501 South Bragaw Street
Anchorage, AK 99507–1599
Phone: 907–786–8500
E-mail: wwapd@ci.anchorage.ak.us

**University of Alaska at Fairbanks Police
Department**
P.O. Box 755560
Fairbanks, AK 99775
Phone: 907–474–7721

Arizona

Maricopa County Attorney's Office
Technology and Electronic Crimes Bureau
301 West Jefferson Street, Fifth Floor
Phoenix, AZ 85003
Phone: 602–506–0139

Office of the Attorney General
Technology Crimes Unit
1275 West Washington Street
Phoenix, AZ 85007
Phone: 602–542–3881
Fax: 602–542–5997
E-mail: ag.inquiries@azag.gov
http://www.azag.gov/cybercrime/

Phoenix Police Department
620 West Washington Street
Phoenix, AZ 85003
Phone: 602–495–0483
http://www.ci.phoenix.az.us/POLICE/

Arkansas

Arkansas State Police
Crimes Against Children Division
#1 State Police Plaza Drive
Little Rock, AR 72209
Phone: 501–618–8386
http://www.asp.state.ar.us/divisions/cac/
  cac_administration.html

Office of the Attorney General
Consumer Protection Division
323 Center Street, Suite 200
Little Rock, AR 72201
Phone: 501–682–2007

**University of Arkansas at Little Rock
Police Department**
2801 South University Avenue
Little Rock, AR 72204
Phone: 501–569–8793/501–569–8794

California

**Bureau of Medi-Cal Fraud and Elder
Abuse**
110 West A Street, Suite 1100
San Diego, CA 92101
Phone: 619–645–2432
Fax: 619–645–2455

California Bureau of Investigation
3046 Prospect Park Drive, Unit 1
Rancho Cordova, CA 95760
Phone: 916–464–2001

California Franchise Tax Board
Investigations Bureau
100 North Barranca Street, Suite 600
West Covina, CA 91791–1600
Phone: 626–859–4678

**Computer And Technology Crime High-Tech Response Team
C.A.T.C.H.**
330 West Broadway, Suite 700
San Diego, CA 92101
http://www.catchteam.org/

Kern County Sheriff's Department
1350 Norris Road
Bakersfield, CA 93308
Phone: 661–391–7500
sheriff@co.kern.ca.us

Los Angeles Police Department
Computer Crime Unit
150 North Los Angeles Street
Los Angeles, CA 90012
Phone: 877–275–5273
E-mail: lapdonline@earthlink.net
http://www.lapdonline.org/

Modesto Police Department
600 10th Street
Modesto, CA 95353
Phone: 209–572–9500

Northern California Computer Crime Task Force
455 Devlin Drive
Napa, CA 94559
Phone: 707–253–4500
http://www.nc3tf.org

Office of the Attorney General
California Department of Justice
1300 I Street, Suite 1101
Sacramento, CA 94244–2550
Phone: 916–445–9555

Office of the Attorney General
California Department of Justice
455 Golden Gate, Suite 11000
San Francisco, CA 94102
Phone: 415–703–1372
(Supports the REACT task force in Santa Clara County/Silicon Valley)

Office of the Attorney General
California Department of Justice
455 Golden Gate, Suite 11000
San Francisco, CA 94102
Phone: 415–703–5868
(Supports the North Bay Task Force covering the SF Bay area)

Office of the Attorney General
California Department of Justice
110 West A Street, Suite 1100
San Diego, CA 92101
Phone: 619–645–2823
(Supports the San Diego Regional Task Force and RCFL)

Regional Computer Forensic Laboratory at San Diego
9797 Aero Drive
San Diego, CA 92123–1800
Phone: 858–499–7799
Fax: 858–499–7798
E-mail: rcfl@rcfl.org
http://www.rcfl.org

Sacramento County Sheriff's Office
Internet Crimes Against Children Task Force
711 G Street
Sacramento, CA 95814
Phone: 916–874–3030
http://www.sachitechcops.org/children.htm

Sacramento Valley Hi-Tech Crimes Task Force
Hi-Tech Crimes Division
Sacramento County Sheriff's Department
P.O. Box 988
Sacramento, CA 95812–0998
Phone: 916–874–3002
E-mail: info@sachitechcops.org
http://www.sachitechcops.org/

San Diego High Technology Crimes Economic Fraud Division
District Attorney's Office, County of San Diego
330 West Broadway
San Diego, CA 92101
Phone: 619–531–4040
Fax: 619–237–1351
E-mail: publicinformation@sdcda.org
http://www.sdcda.org/protecting/
  hightech.php

San Diego Police Department
Internet Crimes Against Children Task Force
9630 Aero Drive
San Diego, CA 92123
Phone: 858–573–0689
E-mail: sdicac@sdicac.org
http://www.sdicac.org/

San Diego Regional Computer Forensic Laboratory Office
9737 Aero Drive (street address)
San Diego, CA 92123
9797 Aero Drive (mailing address)
San Diego, CA 92123
Phone: 858–499–7799
Fax: 858–499–7798
E-mail: rcfl@rcfl.org
http://www.sdrcfl.org/

San Jose Police Department
Silicon Valley Internet Crimes Against
  Children Task Force
201 West Mission Street
San Jose, CA 95110
Phone: 408–277–4102
E-mail: info@svicac.org
http://www.svicac.org/

Silicon Valley High Tech Crime Task Force
Rapid Enforcement Allied Computer Team
  (REACT)
c/o Federal Bureau of Investigation
REACT TASK FORCE
950 South Bascom Avenue, #3011
San Jose, CA 95128
Phone: 408–494–7186
Fax: 408–292–6375
E-mail: reactsj@reacttf.org
http://www.reacttf.org/

Silicon Valley Regional Computer Forensic Laboratory Office
4600 Bohannon Drive, Suite 200
Menlo Park, CA 94025
Phone: 408–795–4314
http://www.svrcfl.org/

Southern California High Technology Crime Task Force
Commercial Crimes Bureau
Los Angeles County Sheriff's Department
11515 South Colima Road, Room M104
Whittier, CA 90604
Phone: 562–946–7942

U.S. Customs Service
Computer Investigative Specialist
3403 10th Street, Suite 600
Riverside, CA 92501

Colorado

Colorado Department of Public Safety
Colorado Bureau of Investigation
690 Kipling Street, Suite 3000
Denver, CO 80215
Phone: 303–239–4679
Fax: 303–274–0217
E-Mail: cbi.denver@cdps.state.co.us

Colorado Springs Police Department
Internet Crimes Against Children Task
  Force
705 South Nevada Avenue
Colorado Springs, CO 80903
Phone: 719–444–7541
http://www.springsgov.com/
  Page.asp?NavID=1480

Denver District Attorney's Office
303 West Colfax Avenue, Suite 1300
Denver, CO 80204
Phone: 720–913–9000
http://www.denverda.org/

Denver Police Department
Computer Crimes Investigations Unit
1331 Cherokee Street
Denver, CO 80204
Phone: 720–913–6168

Office of the Attorney General
1525 Sherman Street, Seventh Floor
Denver, CO 80203
Phone: 303–866–5494

Rocky Mountain Regional Computer Forensic Laboratory Office
1961 Stout Street, Suite 1823
Denver, CO 80294
Phone: 303–629–7171
http://www.rmrcfl.org/

Connecticut

Connecticut Department of Public Safety
Division of Scientific Services
Forensic Science Laboratory
Computer Crimes and Electronic
  Evidence Unit
278 Colony Street
Meriden, CT 06451
Phone: 203–639–6492
Fax: 203– 639-6485
http://www.state.ct.us/dps/

Connecticut Department of Revenue Services
Special Investigations Section
25 Sigourney Street
Hartford, CT 06106
Phone: 860–297–5877
Fax: 860–297–5625
E-mail: DRS@po.state.ct.us

Connecticut State Police
Computer Crimes and Electronic
  Evidence Unit
278 Colony Street
Meriden, CT 06451
Phone: 203–639–6492
http://www.state.ct.us/dps

Office of the Chief State's Attorney
300 Corp. Place
Rocky Hill, CT 06067
Phone: 860–258–5800

Yale University Police Department
98–100 Sachem Street
New Haven, CT 06511
Phone: 203–432–7958
http://www.yale.edu/police/department.
  html#ITS/

Delaware

Delaware State Police
High Technology Crimes Unit
1575 Mckee Road, Suite 204
Dover, DE 19904
Phone: 302–739–5901
Fax: 302–739–1398
http://www.state.de.us/dsp

New Castle County Police Department
Criminal Investigations Unit
3601 North DuPont Highway
  (street address)
New Castle, DE 19720
87 Reads Way (mailing address)
New Castle, DE 19720
Phone: 302–395–8110

Office of the Attorney General
Criminal Division
820 North French Street, Seventh Floor
Wilmington, DE 19801
Phone: 302–577–8500

University of Delaware Police Department
101 MOB
700 Pilottown Road
Lewes, DE 19958
Phone: 302–831–2222
E-mail: publicsafety@udel.edu
http://128.175.24.251/

District of Columbia

Metropolitan Police Department
Special Investigations Division
Computer Crimes and Forensics Unit
300 Indiana Avenue N.W., Room 3016
Washington, DC 20001
Phone: 202–727–7003

Florida

Broward County Sheriff's Office
2601 West Broward Boulevard
Ft. Lauderdale, FL 33312
Phone: 954–888–5256
E-mail: www.leachtaskforce@sheriff.org
http://www.sheriff.org

Florida Atlantic University Police Department
777 Glades Road, #69
Boca Raton, FL 33431
Phone: 561–297–3500
Fax: 561–297–3565

Florida Department of Law Enforcement
Computer Crime Center
P.O. Box 1489
Tallahassee, FL 32302
Phone: 850–410–7060

Gainesville Police Department
P.O. Box 1250
721 North West Sixth Street
Gainesville, FL 32602
Phone: 352–334–2561/352–334–2488
http://www.gainesvillepd.org

Institute of Police Technology and Management
Computer Forensics Laboratory
University of North Florida
12000 Alumni Drive
Jacksonville, FL 32224–2678
Phone: 904–620–4786
Fax: 904–620–2453
http://www.iptm.org/crim.htm#026119

Office of Statewide Prosecution
High Technology Crimes
135 West Central Boulevard, Suite 1000
Orlando, FL 32801
Phone: 407–245–0893
Fax: 407–245–0356
http://myfloridalegal.com/pages.nsf/4492D
    797DC0BD92F85256CB80055FB97/18A
    7753257FE439085256CC9004EC4F7?
    OpenDocument

Pinellas County Sheriff's Office
10750 Ulmerton Road
Largo, FL 33778
Phone: 727–582–6200

Georgia

Georgia Bureau of Investigation
Financial Investigations Unit
3121 Panthersville Road
P.O. Box 370808
Decatur, Georgia 30037–0808
Phone: 404–212–4050
http://www.ganet.org/gbi

Office of the Attorney General
40 Capital Square
135 State Judicial Building
Atlanta, GA 30334–1300
Phone: 404–656–5959

Hawaii

Hawaii Department of the Attorney General
425 Queen Street
Honolulu, HI 96813
Phone: 808–586–1171/808–586–1240

Hawaii Department of the Attorney General
Hawaii Internet Crimes Against Children
 Task Force
235 South Beretania Street, 16th Floor
Honolulu, HI 96813
Phone: 808–587–4114
E-mail: atg_icac@hawaii.gov
http://www.hawaii.gov/ag/hicac/index.htm

Honolulu Police Department
White Collar Crime Unit
801 South Beretania Street
Honolulu, HI 96819
Phone: 808–529–3112

Idaho

Ada County Sheriff's Office
7200 Barrister Drive
Boise, ID 83704
Phone: 208–377–6691

Office of the Attorney General
Criminal Division
700 West Jefferson Street, Room 210
Boise, ID 83720
Phone: 208–332–3096

Illinois

Chicago Regional Computer Forensic Laboratory Office
610 South Canal Street
Chicago, IL 60607
Phone: 312–913–9270
Fax: 312–913–9408
http://www.chicagorcfl.org/

Illinois State Police
Computer Crimes Investigation Unit
Division of Operations
Operational Services Command
Statewide Special Investigations Bureau
500 Illes Park Place, Suite 104
Springfield, IL 62703
Phone: 217–785–0631
Fax: 217–785–6793

Illinois State Police
Computer Crimes Investigation Unit
9511 West Harrison Street
Des Plaines, IL 60016–1562
Phone: 847–294–4400

Office of the Attorney General
High Tech Crimes Bureau
100 West Randolph Street, 12th Floor
Chicago, IL 60601
Phone: 312–814–3762
State of Illinois High Tech Crimes Network
http://www.hightechcrimes.net/

Tazewell County State's Attorney CID
Regional Computer Crime Enforcement
 Group, Team 1
342 Court Street, Suite 6
Pekin, IL 61554–3298
Phone: 309–477–2205, ext. 400
Fax: 309–477–2205

Indiana

Evansville Police Department
15 N.W. Martin Luther King, Jr. Boulevard
Evansville, IN 47708
Phone: 812–436–7995/812–436–7994
http://www.evansvillepolice.com/computer_
 department.htm

Indiana State Police
North Central Indiana CyberCrime
 Investigations
501 South Adams Street
Marion, IN 46953
Phone: 765–662–9864
E-mail: cybercrime@grantcounty.net
http://operations.grant.in.uinquire.us/
 nxweb.exe?PAGEID=0013

Indiana State Police
Government Center North
100 North Senate, Room 314
Indianapolis, IN 46204
Phone: 317–247–1852
http://www.in.gov/isp/bci/criminal/special.
html

**Indianapolis Police Department
Training Academy**
901 North Post Road, Room 115
Indianapolis, IN 46219
Phone: 317–327–3461
E-mail: vulcan@netdirect.net
http://www.indygov.org/eGov/City/DPS/IPD/
Enforcement/Investigations/org-crime.htm

Marion Police Department
Computer Crime Investigations and
  Forensic Lab
301 South Branson Street
Marion, IN 46952
Phone: 765–662–9981

Office of the Attorney General
402 West Washington Street
Indianapolis, IN 46204
Phone: 317–232–6239

Iowa

Iowa Division of Criminal Investigation
502 East Ninth Street
Des Moines, IA 50319
Phone: 515–281–3666
Fax: 515–242–6297

Office of the Attorney General
1305 East Walnut Street
Des Moines, IA 50319
Phone: 515–281–5164

Kansas

Kansas Bureau of Investigation
High Technology Crime Investigation Unit
1620 S.W. Tyler Street
Topeka, KS 66612–1837
Phone: 785–296–8222
Fax: 785–296–0525

Olathe Police Department
501 East 56 Highway
Olathe, KS 66061
Phone: 913–782–4500

Sedgwick County Sheriff's Office
130 South Market
Wichita, KS 67202
Phone: 316–337–6562
http://www.sedgwickcounty.org/emcu

Wichita Police Department
Forensic Computer Crimes Unit
455 North Main, Sixth Floor Lab
Wichita, KS 67202
Phone: 316–337–6552
E-mail: forensics@kscable.com

Kentucky

Boone County Sheriff
P.O. Box 198
Burlington, KY 41005
Phone: 859–334–2175

Kentucky State Police
1240 Airport Road
Frankfort, KY 40601
Phone: 502–226–2160
http://www.kentuckystatepolice.org

Office of the Attorney General
Special Prosecutions Division
1024 Capitol Center Drive
Frankfort, KY 40601
Phone: 502–696–5337

Louisiana

Gonzales Police Department
120 South Irma Boulevard
Gonzales, LA 70737
Phone: 225–647–2841
Fax: 225–647–9544
E-mail: vsmith@leo.gov

Louisiana Department of Justice
High Technology Crime Unit
P.O. Box 94095
Baton Rouge, LA 70804
Phone: 225–342–7552
E-mail: HTCU@ag.state.la.us
http://www.ag.state.la.us/HighTech.aspx

Louisiana Department of Justice
Louisiana Internet Crimes Against Children
 Task Force
339 Florida Street, Suite 402
Baton Rouge, LA 70801
Phone: 225–342–0921
http://www.ag.state.la.us/icac.aspx

Maine

Maine Computer Crimes Task Force
171 Park Street
Lewiston, ME 04240
Phone: 207–784–6422

Maine Computer Crimes Task Force
15 Oak Grove Road
Vassalboro, ME 04989
Phone: 207–877–8081

Office of the Attorney General
Computer Crimes Task Force
44 Oak Street, 4th Floor
Portland, ME 04101
Phone: 207–626–8800

Maryland

Anne Arundel County Police Department
Computer Crimes Unit
41 Community Place
Crownsville, MD 21032
Phone: 410–222–3419
Fax: 410–987–7433

Maryland Department of State Police
Computer Crimes Unit
Unit Commander
7155–C Columbia Gateway Drive
Columbia, MD 21046
Phone: 410–290–1620
Fax: 410–290–1831
http://ccu.mdsp.org/home.htm

Maryland Department of State Police
Internet Crimes Against Children
 Task Force
7155 Columbia Gateway Drive
Columbia, MD 21046
Phone: 410–977–4519
E-mail: icac@mdsp.org
http://icac.mdsp.org

Montgomery County Police
Computer Crime Unit
2350 Research Boulevard
Rockville, MD 20850
Phone: 301–840–2590
E-mail: CCU@co.mo.md.us
http://www.montgomerycountymd.gov/
 poltmpl.asp?url=/Content/POL/ask/
 computerCrimes.asp

Office of the Attorney General
Criminal Investigations Division
200 South Paul Place
Baltimore, MD 21202
Phone: 410–576–6380

Massachusetts

Massachusetts State Police
340 West Brookfield Road
New Braintree, MA 01531
Phone: 508–867–1080

Office of the Attorney General
High Tech and Computer Crime Division
One Ashburton Place
Boston, MA 02108
Phone: 617–727–2200
http://www.ago.state.ma.us/
 sp.cfm?pageid=1198

Michigan

Michigan Department of the Attorney General
High Tech Crime Unit
18050 Deering
Livonia, MI 48152
Phone: 734–525–4151
Fax: 734–525–4372
http://www.michigan.gov/ag

Michigan State Police
Internet Crimes Against Children
 Task Force
4000 Collins Road
Lansing, MI 48909
Phone: 517–336–6444
http://www.michigan.gov/ag/0,1607,7-164-
 17334_18155-46048—,00.html

Oakland County Sheriff's Department
Computer Crimes Unit
1201 North Telegraph Road
Pontiac, MI 48341
Phone: 248–858–4942
Fax: 248–858–9565
E-mail: ocso@oakgov.com
http://www.oakgov.com/sheriff

Minnesota

Department of Public Safety
Bureau of Criminal Apprehension
1246 University
St. Paul, MN 55104–4197
Phone: 651–642–0610

Office of the Attorney General
Criminal Division
525 Park Street, Suite 500
St. Paul, MN 55103
Phone: 651–297–1050

Ramsey County Sheriff's Department
14 West Kellogg Boulevard
St. Paul, MN 55102
Phone: 651–266–2797

St. Paul Police Department
Minnesota Internet Crimes Against
 Children Task Force
367 Grove Street, Second Floor
Saint Paul, MN 55101
Phone: 651–266–5882
E-mail: micac@ci.stpaul.mn.us
http://www.ci.stpaul.mn.us/depts/police/
 icac/icac.html

Mississippi

Biloxi Police Department
170 Porter Avenue
Biloxi, MS 39530
Phone: 228–435–6100
Fax: 228–374–1922

Office of the Attorney General
Public Integrity Section
P.O. Box 2
Jackson, MS 39205
Phone: 601–359–4250

Missouri

Heart of America Regional Computer Forensic Laboratory Office
4150 North Mulberry Drive, Suite 250
Kansas City, MO 64116–1696
Phone: 816–584–4300
http://www.harcfl.org/

Office of the Attorney General
High Tech Crimes Unit
207 West High
Jefferson City, MO 65101
Phone: 573–751–3321

Office of the Attorney General
High Tech Crime Unit
1530 Rax Court
Jefferson City, MO 65109
Phone: 816–889–5000

St. Louis Metropolitan Police Department
High Tech Crimes Unit
Sex Crimes and Child Abuse Unit
1200 Clark
St. Louis, MO 63103
Phone: 314–444–5441
http://stlcin.missouri.org/circuitattorney/
sexcrimes.cfm

Montana

Montana Division of Criminal Investigation
Computer Crime Unit
303 North Roberts, Room 371
Helena, MT 59620
Phone: 406–444–3874
E-mail: contactdoj@state.mt.us

Office of the Attorney General
Legal Services Division
215 North Sanders
Helena, MT 59620
Phone: 406–444–2026

Office of the Attorney General
Computer Crime Unit
303 North Roberts, Room 361
Helena, MT 59620
Phone: 406–444–3875

Nebraska

Lincoln Police Department
575 South 10th Street
Lincoln, NE 68508
Phone: 402–441–7587
E-mail: lpd@cjis.ci.lincoln.ne.us

Nebraska State Patrol
Internet Crimes Against Children Unit
4411 South 108th Street
Omaha, NE 68137
Phone: 402–595–2410
Fax: 402–595–3303
http://www.nsp.state.ne.us/
findfile.asp?id2=52

Office of the Attorney General
2115 State Capitol
P.O. Box 98930
Lincoln, NE 68509
Phone: 402–471–4794

Nevada

City of Reno Police Department
Computer Crimes Unit
455 East Second Street (street address)
Reno, NV 89502
P.O. Box 1900 (mailing address)
Reno, NV 89505
Phone: 775–334–2107
Fax: 775–785–4026

Las Vegas Metropolitan Police Department
Las Vegas Regional Internet Crimes
Against Children Task Force
3010 West Charleston, #120
Las Vegas, NV 89102
Phone: 702–229–3599
http://www.lvicac.com

Office of the Attorney General
100 North Carson Street
Carson City, NV 89701
Phone: 775–684–1100

Office of the Attorney General
Nevada Cyber Crime Task Force
5420 Kietzke Lane, Suite 202
Reno, NV 89511
Phone: 775–688–1818

New Hampshire

New Hampshire State Police Forensic Laboratory
Computer Crimes Unit
10 Hazen Drive
Concord, NH 03305
Phone: 603–271–0300
http://www.state.nh.us/safety/infotech/
index.html

Office of the Attorney General
33 Capitol Street
Concord, NH 03301–6397
Phone: 603–271–3671

Office of Juvenile Justice and Delinquency Prevention
Internet Crimes Against Children Task Force Training and Technical Assistance
University of New Hampshire
Crimes Against Children Research Center, West Edge
7 Leavitt Lane
Durham, NH 03824
Phone: 603–862–7031
http://www.unh.edu/ccrc/NJOV_info_
page.htm

Portsmouth Police Department
Internet Crimes Against Children Task Force
3 Junkins Avenue
Portsmouth, NH 03801
Phone: 603–427–1500
http://www.ci.keene.nh.us/police/task_
force.htm

New Jersey

New Jersey Division of Criminal Justice
Computer Analysis and Technology Unit
25 Market Street
P.O. Box 085
Trenton, NJ 08625–0085
Phone: 609–984–5256/609–984–6500
http://www.state.nj.us/lps/dcj/catu/
catunit.htm

New Jersey Regional Computer Forensic Laboratory Office
NJSP Technology Center
1200 Negron Drive
Hamilton, NJ 08691
Phone: 609–584–5051, ext. 5676
http://www.njrcfl.org/

New Jersey State Police
High Tech Crimes Unit
P.O. Box 7068
West Trenton, NJ 08628
Phone: 609–882–2000, ext. 2904
http://www.njsp.org

Ocean County Prosecutor's Office
Special Investigations Unit/
  Computer Crimes
P.O. Box 2191
Toms River, NJ 08754
Phone: 732–929–2027, ext. 4014
Fax: 732–240–3338

New Mexico

New Mexico Gaming Control Board
Information Systems Division
6400 Uptown Boulevard N.E., Suite 100E
Albuquerque, NM 87110
Phone: 505–841–9719
http://www.nmgcb.org/divisions/
  infosys

Office of the Attorney General
P.O. Drawer 1508
Sante Fe, NM 87504–1508
Phone: 505–827–6000

Office of the Attorney General
111 Lomas N.W., Suite 300
Albuquerque, NM 87102
Phone: 505–222–9000

Twelfth Judicial District Attorney's Office
1000 New York Avenue, Room 301
Alamogordo, NM 88310
Phone: 505–437–3640, ext. 110

New York

Erie County Sheriff's Office
Computer Crime Unit
134 West Eagle
Buffalo, NY 14202
Phone: 716–858–6889
http://www.erie.gov/sheriff/ccu.asp

Nassau County Police Department
Computer Crime Section
970 Brush Hollow Road
Westbury, NY 11590
Phone: 516–573–5275

New York State Attorney General's Office
Internet Bureau
120 Broadway
New York, NY 10271
Phone: 212–416–6344
http://www.oag.state.ny.us/internet/
  internet.html

New York State Department of Taxation and Finance
Office of Deputy Inspector General
Building 9, Room 481
Albany, NY 12227
Phone: 518–485–8698

New York State Police
Computer Crime Unit
Forensic Investigation Center
Building 30, State Campus
1220 Washington Avenue
Albany, NY 12226
Phone: 518–457–5712
Fax: 518–402–2773
E-mail: nyspccu@troopers.state.ny.us
http://www.troopers.state.ny.us/Criminal_
  Investigation/Computer_Crimes/
http://www.troopers.state.ny.us/Criminal_
  Investigation/Internet_Crimes_Against_
  Children

Rockland County Sheriff's Department
Computer Crime Task Force
27 New Hempstead Road
New City, NY 10956
Phone: 845–708–7860/845–638–5836
Fax: 845–708–7821
E-mail: info@rocklandcomputercops.com

North Carolina

North Carolina State Bureau of Investigation
P.O. Box 25099
Raleigh, NC 27611
Phone: 919–716–0000
http://www.ncsbi.gov

Office of the Attorney General
Law Enforcement and Prosecution Division
P.O. Box 629
Raleigh, NC 27602
Phone: 919–716–6500

Raleigh Police Department
110 South McDowell Street
Raleigh, NC 27601
Phone: 919–890–3555

North Dakota

North Dakota Bureau of Criminal Investigation
Cybercrime Unit
P.O. Box 1054
Bismarck, ND 58502–1054
Phone: 701–328–5500
E-mail: BCIinfo@state.nd.us

Ohio

Cuyahoga County Prosecutor's Office
1200 Ontario Street, Ninth Floor
Cleveland, OH 44115
Phone: 216–443–7825
http://prosecutor.cuyahogacounty.us/
  internet_safety.asp

Hamilton County Ohio Sheriff's Office
Justice Center
1000 Sycamore Street, Room 110
Cincinnati, OH 45202
Phone: 513–946–6685
Fax: 513–946–6690
http://www.hcso.org

Miami Valley Regional Computer Forensic Laboratory Office
Federal Building
200 West Second Street
Dayton, OH 45402
Phone: 937–512–1913
Fax: 937–512–1950
http://www.mvrcfl.org/

Office of the Attorney General
Bureau of Criminal Investigation
Computer Crime Unit
1560 State Route 56
London, OH 43140
Phone: 740–845–2410

Office of the Attorney General
Computer Crime Task Force
140 East Town Street, 14th Floor
Columbus, OH 43215–6001
Phone: 614–644–7233

Riverside Police Department
1791 Harshman Road
Riverside, OH 45424
Phone: 937–233–1801
E-mail: police@riverside.oh.us

Oklahoma

Oklahoma Attorney General
4545 North Lincoln Boulevard, Suite 260
Oklahoma City, OK 73105–3498
Phone: 405–521–4274
E-mail: okoag@oag.state.ok.us

Oklahoma State Bureau of Investigation
Computer Crime Unit
6600 North Harvey
Oklahoma City, OK 73116
Phone: 405–427–5421
http://www.osbi.state.ok.us/Inv.html

Oregon

Eugene Police Department
Financial Crimes Unit
777 Pearl Street, Room 107
Eugene, OR 97401
Phone: 541–682–2682

Northwest Regional Computer Forensic Laboratory Office
1201 Northeast Lloyd Boulevard, Suite 600
Portland, OR 97237
Phone: 503–224–4181
http://www.nwrcfl.org/

Office of the Attorney General
1162 Court Street N.E.
Salem, OR 97301
Phone: 503–378–6347

Portland Police Bureau
Computer Crimes Detail
1115 S.W. Second Avenue
Portland, OR 97204
Phone: 503–823–0871

Washington County Sheriff's Office
215 S.W. Adams Avenue, MS32
Hillsboro, OR 97123
Phone: 503–846–2733
Fax: 503–846–2637
http://www.co.washington.or.us/sheriff/
   investig/fraud.htm

Pennsylvania

Allegheny County Police Department
High Tech Crime Unit
400 North Lexington Street
Pittsburgh, PA 15208
Phone: 412–473–3000
Fax: 412–473–3332

Delaware County District Attorney's Office
Internet Crimes Against Children
 Task Force
Media Courthouse CID
Media, PA 19063
Phone: 610–891–4709
http://www.delcoicac.com/home.html

Erie County District Attorney's Office
Erie County Courthouse
140 West Sixth Street
Erie, PA 16501
Phone: 814–451–6349
Fax: 814–451–6419

Office of Attorney General
Computer Forensics Unit
106 Lowthar Street
Lemoyne, PA 17043
Phone: 717–712–2023

Office of Attorney General
Computer Forensics Section
2490 Boulevard of the Generals
Norristown, PA 19403
Phone: 610–631–5937

Pennsylvania State Police
Computer Crimes Unit
1800 Elmerton Avenue
Harrisburg, PA 17110
Phone: 717–772–7631

Rhode Island
Department of the Attorney General
Criminal Division
150 South Main Street
Providence, RI 02903
Phone: 401–274–4400

Warwick Police Department
BCI Unit, Detective Division
99 Veterans Memorial Drive
Warwick, RI 02886
Phone: 401–468–4200
E-mail:WPDDetectives@warwickri.com

South Carolina

South Carolina Attorney General's Office
Internet Crimes Against Children
P.O. Box 11549
Columbia, SC 29211
Phone: 803–734–6151
E-mail: info@sckidsonline.com
http://www.sckidsonline.com

South Carolina Law Enforcement Division
P.O. Box 21398
Columbia, SC 29221–1398
Phone: 803–896–2277
http://www.sled.state.sc.us/

Winthrop University Campus Police
Department of Public Safety
02 Crawford Building
Rock Hill, SC 29733
Phone: 803–323–3333

South Dakota

Office of the Attorney General
500 East Capital
Pierre, SD 57501–5070
Phone: 605–773–3215

Office of the Attorney General
Criminal Division
Box 70
Robin City, SD 57709
Phone: 605–394–2258

Tennessee

Harriman Police Department
130 Pansy Hill Road
Harriman, TN 37748
Phone: 865–882–3383
Fax: 865–882–0700
E-mail: crimeseen@earthlink.net

Knox County Sheriff's Office
400 West Main Avenue
Knoxville, TN 37902
Phone: 865–971–3911
E-mail: sheriff@esper.com

Knoxville Police Department
Internet Crimes Against Children
800 Howard Baker, Jr. Avenue
Knoxville, TN 37915
Phone: 865–215–7020
http://www.ci.knoxville.tn.us/kpd/
  crimesvschildren.asp

Office of the Attorney General
Computer Forensic Unit
425 Fifth Avenue, North
Nashville, TN 37243
Phone: 615–532–5817

Office of the Attorney General
500 Charlotte Avenue
Nashville, TN 37243
Phone: 615–741–4082

Texas

Austin Police Department
715 East Eighth Street
Austin, TX 78701
Phone: 512–974–5000

Bexar County District Attorney's Office
300 Dolorosa
San Antonio, TX 78205
Phone: 210–335–2974/210–335–2991
http://www.co.bexar.tx.us/da2/

Dallas Police Department
Computer Crimes Team
1400 South Lamar Street
Dallas, TX 75215
Phone: 214–671–3503
http://www.dallaspolice.net/index.
  cfm?page_ID=4054&subnav=55

Dallas Police Department
Child Exploitation Unit
1400 South Lamar Street, Room 3N061
Dallas, TX 75215
Phone: 214–671–4211
http://www.dallaspolice.net/index.
  cfm?page_ID=3114

Federal Bureau of Investigation
Dallas Field Office
One Justice Way
Dallas, TX 75220
Phone: 972–559–5000
E-mail: Dallas@FBI.gov
http://dallas.fbi.gov/dala.htm

**Greater Houston Regional Computer
Forensic Laboratory Office**
2900 North Loop West, Ninth Floor
Houston, TX 77092
Phone: 713–316–7878
http://www.ghrcfl.org/

Houston Police Department
1200 Travis Street
Houston, TX 77002
Phone: 713–884–3131

**North Texas Regional Computer
Forensic Laboratory Office**
301 North Market Street, #500
Dallas, TX 75202–1878
Phone: 972–559–5800
Fax: 972–559–5880
http://www.ntrcfl.org/

Office of the Attorney General
Cyber Crimes Unit
P.O. Box 12548
Austin, TX 78711–2548
Phone: 512–936–2899

Portland Police Department
902 Moore Avenue
Portland, TX 78374
Phone: 361–643–2546
Fax: 361–643–5689

Texas Department of Public Safety
5805 North Lamar Boulevard
  (street address)
Austin, TX 78752–4422
P.O. Box 4087 (mailing address)
Austin, TX 78773–0001
Phone: 512–424–2200/800–252–5402
E-mail: specialcrimes@txdps.state.tx.us
http://www.txdps.state.tx.us/ccrime.htm

Utah

Intermountain West Regional Computer Forensic Laboratory Office
257 East 200 South, Suite 1200
Salt Lake City, UT 84111
Phone: 801–579–1400
http://www.iwrcfl.org/

Utah Department of Public Safety
Criminal Investigations Bureau,
  Forensic Computer Lab
5272 South College Drive, Suite 200
Murray, UT 84123
Phone: 801–955–2100
http://sbi.utah.gov/compforensic/

Utah Office of Attorney General
Utah Internet Crimes Against Children
  Task Force
257E 200 South, Suite 1200
Salt Lake City, UT 84111
Phone: 801–579–4530
http://attorneygeneral.utah.gov/ICAC/
  icacmain.htm

Vermont

Chittenden Unit for Special Investigations
Internet Crimes Against Children
  Task Force
50 Cherry Street, Suite 102
Burlington, VT 05401
Phone: 802–652–6800

Office of the Attorney General
109 State Street
Montpelier, VT 05609-1001
Phone: 802–828–5512

State of Vermont Department of Public Safety
Bureau of Criminal Investigation
103 South Main Street
Waterbury, VT 05671–2101
Phone: 802–244–8721/800–347–0488
Fax: 802–241–5349
http://www.dps.state.vt.us/vtsp/
  computer.html

Vermont Internet Crimes Task Force
1 North Avenue
Burlington, VT 05401
Phone: 802–857–0092
E-mail:info@vtinternetcrimes.org
http://www.vtinternetcrimes.org/

Virginia

Arlington County Police Department
Criminal Investigations Division
Computer Forensics
1425 North Courthouse Road
Arlington, VA 22201
Phone: 703–228–4239

Bedford County Sheriff's Office
Internet Crimes Against Children Task
  Force
1345 Falling Creek Road
Bedford, VA 24523
Phone: 540–586–4800
http://www.blueridgethunder.com

Fairfax County Police Department
Computer Forensics Section
4100 Chain Bridge Road
Fairfax, VA 22030
Phone: 703–246–7800
Fax: 703–246–4253

National Center for Missing & Exploited Children
699 Prince Street
Alexandria, VA 22314
Phone: 703–837–6337
http://www.missingkids.com

Office of the Attorney General
Computer Crime Unit
900 East Main Street
Richmond, VA 23219
Phone: 804–659–3122

Regional Computer Forensic Laboratory National Program Office
Engineering Research Facility
Attn: RCFL National Program Office
Building 27958–A
Quantico, VA 22135
Phone: 703–902–5502
E-mail: info@nationalrcfl.org
http://www.rcfl.gov/

Richmond Police Department
Technology Crimes Section
200 West Grace Street
Richmond, VA 23220
Phone: 804–646–3949

Virginia Beach Police Department
Special Investigations CERU
2509 Princess Anne Road
Virginia Beach, VA 23456
Phone: 757–427–1749
http://www.vbgov.com/dept/police/

Virginia Department of Motor Vehicles
Law Enforcement Section
Assistant Special Agent in Charge
945 Edwards Ferry Road
Leesburg, VA 20175
Phone: 703–771–4757

Virginia State Police
High Tech Crimes Unit
P.O. Box 27472
Richmond, VA 23261
Phone: 804–674–2000
http://www.vsp.state.va.us/

Washington

King County Sheriff's Office
Fraud/Computer Forensic Unit
401 Fourth Avenue North, RJC 104
Kent, WA 98032–4429
Phone: 206–296–4280
http://www.metrokc.gov/sheriff/what/
　investigations/fraud.aspx

Lynnwood Police Department
High Tech Property Crimes
19321 44th Avenue West (street address)
P.O. Box 5008 (mailing address)
Lynnwood, WA 98046–5008
Phone: 425–744–6900
Fax: 425–672–6835
E-mail: kmanser@ci.lynnwood.wa.us

Office of the Attorney General
High Tech Crimes Unit
900 Fourth Avenue, Suite 2000
Seattle, WA 98164
Phone: 206–464–6430

Seattle Police Department
Internet Crimes Against Children Task
　Force
610 Fifth Avenue
Seattle, WA 98104
Phone: 206–684–4351
http://www.cityofseattle.net/police/
　Programs/ICAC/icac.htm

Tacoma Police Department
PCSO
930 Tacoma Avenue South
Tacoma, WA 98402
Phone: 253–591–5679
E-mail: info@TacomaPolice.org

Vancouver Police Department
Computer Forensics Specialist
300 East 13th Street
Vancouver, WA 98660
Phone: 360–735–8887
E-mail: ecrimes@ci.vancouver.wa.us

Washington State Department of Fish and Wildlife
600 Capitol Way North
Olympia, WA 98501
Phone: 360–902–2276

Washington State Patrol
Computer Forensics Unit
P.O. Box 2347
Airdustrial Way, Building 17
Olympia, WA 98507–2347
Phone: 360–753–3277
http://www.wsp.wa.gov/crime/iad.htm

West Virginia

Office of the Attorney General
P.O. Box 1789
Charleston, WV 25326–1789
Phone: 304–558–8986

Wisconsin

Green Bay Police Department
307 South Adams Street
Phone: 920–448–3200
Green Bay, WI 54301
http://www.gbpolice.org/inv/
  detectives.html

Madison Police Department
211 South Carroll Street
Madison, WI 53709
Phone: 608–267–8824/608–266–4022

Wisconsin Department of Justice
Computer Crimes Unit
P.O. Box 7857
Madison, WI 53707–7851
Phone: 608–266–1221

Wisconsin Department of Justice
Division of Criminal Investigation
17 West Main Street
Madison, WI 53702
Phone: 608–267–1326
http://www.doj.state.wi.us/dci/
  tech/#internet

Wood County Sheriff's Department
400 Market Street
Wis Rapids, WI 54495
Phone: 715–421–8700
E-mail: wcsd@tznet.com

Wyoming

Casper Police Department
201 North David
Casper, WY 82601
Phone: 307–235–8225

Gillette Police Department
201 East Fifth Street
Gillette, WY 82716
Phone: 307–682–5109
E-mail: lenf@ci.gillette.wy.us

Green River Police Department
50 East Second North
Green River, WY 82935
Phone: 307–872–0555
E-mail: tjarvie@cityofgreenriver.org;
  dhyer@cityofgreenriver.org

Wyoming Division of Criminal Investigation
316 West 22nd Street
Cheyenne, WY 82002
Phone: 307–777–7183
Fax: 307–777–7252
http://attorneygeneral.state.wy.us/dci/
  compfaq.html

Wyoming Division of Criminal Investigation
Wyoming Internet Crimes Against Children
  Task Force
316 West 22nd Street
Cheyenne, WY 82002
Phone: 307–777–7806
http://wyomingicac.net

Appendix J. Legal Resources List

American Prosecutors Research Institute
99 Canal Center Plaza, Suite 510
Alexandria, VA 22314
Phone: 703–549–9222
Fax: 703–836–3195
http://www.ndaa-apri.org/apri/

National Association of Attorneys General
750 First Street N.E., Suite 1100
Washington, DC 20002
Phone: 202–326–6000
Fax: 202–408–7014
http://www.naag.org

U.S. Department of Justice
Computer Crime and Intellectual Property
  Section
10th & Constitution Avenue N.W.
John C. Keeney Building, Suite 600
Washington, DC 20530
Phone: 202–514–1026
http://www.cybercrime.gov

Appendix K. List of Organizations

The following is a list of organizations to which a draft copy of this document was mailed.

Alaska Criminal Laboratory

America Online–Investigations and Law Enforcement Affairs

American Prosecutors Research Institute

American Society of Law Enforcement Trainers

Bureau of Alcohol, Tobacco, Firearms and Explosives–Computer Forensics Branch

Center for Law and Computers, Chicago-Kent College of Law, Illinois Institute of Technology

Chicago Regional Computer Forensics Laboratory

Computer Forensics Inc.

Computer Science and Telecommunications Board

Criminal Justice Institute

Drug Enforcement Administration–Digital Evidence Laboratory

Federal Bar Association

Federal Bureau of Investigation

Federal Law Enforcement Training Center–Financial Fraud Institute

Georgia Bureau of Investigation, Intelligence Unit

Hawaii County Police

Heart of America Regional Computer Forensics Laboratory

Intermountain West Regional Computer Forensics Laboratory

Miami Valley Regional Computer Forensics Laboratory

The MITRE Corporation

National Center for Forensic Science

National Computer Security Association (TruSecure)

National Law Enforcement and Corrections Technology Center–West

New Jersey Regional Computer Forensics Laboratory

North Texas Regional Computer Forensics Laboratory

Northwest Regional Computer Forensics Laboratory

Ohio Bureau of Criminal ID and Investigation

Regional Computer Forensic Laboratory National Program Office

Rocky Mountain Regional Computer Forensics Laboratory

San Diego Regional Computer Forensic Laboratory

Silicon Valley Regional Computer Forensic Laboratory

Social Security Administration–Office of the Inspector General, Office of Investigations

U.S. Department of Defense Cyber Crime Center

U.S. Department of Justice–Computer Crime and Intellectual Property Section

U.S. Department of Justice–Western District of Michigan

U.S. Naval Criminal Investigative Service

U.S. Postal Service, Office of Inspector General

About the National Institute of Justice

NIJ is the research, development, and evaluation agency of the U.S. Department of Justice. NIJ's mission is to advance scientific research, development, and evaluation to enhance the administration of justice and public safety. NIJ's principal authorities are derived from the Omnibus Crime Control and Safe Streets Act of 1968, as amended (see 42 U.S.C. §§ 3721–3723).

The NIJ Director is appointed by the President and confirmed by the Senate. The Director establishes the Institute's objectives, guided by the priorities of the Office of Justice Programs, the U.S. Department of Justice, and the needs of the field. The Institute actively solicits the views of criminal justice and other professionals and researchers to inform its search for the knowledge and tools to guide policy and practice.

Strategic Goals

NIJ has seven strategic goals grouped into three categories:

Creating relevant knowledge and tools

1. Partner with State and local practitioners and policymakers to identify social science research and technology needs.
2. Create scientific, relevant, and reliable knowledge—with a particular emphasis on terrorism, violent crime, drugs and crime, cost-effectiveness, and community-based efforts—to enhance the administration of justice and public safety.
3. Develop affordable and effective tools and technologies to enhance the administration of justice and public safety.

Dissemination

4. Disseminate relevant knowledge and information to practitioners and policymakers in an understandable, timely, and concise manner.
5. Act as an honest broker to identify the information, tools, and technologies that respond to the needs of stakeholders.

Agency management

6. Practice fairness and openness in the research and development process.
7. Ensure professionalism, excellence, accountability, cost-effectiveness, and integrity in the management and conduct of NIJ activities and programs.

Program Areas

In addressing these strategic challenges, the Institute is involved in the following program areas: crime control and prevention, including policing; drugs and crime; justice systems and offender behavior, including corrections; violence and victimization; communications and information technologies; critical incident response; investigative and forensic sciences, including DNA; less-than-lethal technologies; officer protection; education and training technologies; testing and standards; technology assistance to law enforcement and corrections agencies; field testing of promising programs; and international crime control.

In addition to sponsoring research and development and technology assistance, NIJ evaluates programs, policies, and technologies. NIJ communicates its research and evaluation findings through conferences and print and electronic media.

To find out more about the National Institute of Justice, please visit:

http://www.ojp.usdoj.gov/nij

or contact:

National Criminal Justice
 Reference Service
P.O. Box 6000
Rockville, MD 20849–6000
800–851–3420
e-mail: *askncjrs@ncjrs.org*